Advance Praise for

STRIKE THE BABY
and KILL THE BLONDE

"For every person who ever wondered just what, exactly, a grip [...]
grips. . . . This comprehensive glossary of cinematic lingo is as much [...]
for the filmmaker as it is the filmgoer."

—JANE ROSENTHAL, producer
(Analyze That, Meet the Parents, About a Boy)

"Dave Knox's book is much more than a definition of film terms. It
offers a dead-on look at the film business and life on a movie set, with
an insight that is both authentic and funny."

—ROBIN SQUIBB, script supervisor
(Hitch, Analyze This, Die Hard III)

" 'FO the double and gimme a lavender' makes perfect sense to a grip
but is impenetrable nonsense to the layman. Now with this lucid and
amusing guide to the particular argot of the movie business, the out-
sider can begin to understand what it all means."

—MICHAEL CHAPMAN, director of photography
(Raging Bull, Taxi Driver, The Fugitive, Space Jam)

"I only wish that this book had been written thirty years ago, when as
an immigrant cameraman I landed in New York and tried to work in a
new language. I was perplexed, and *Strike the Baby* would have provided some answers not found in standard dictionaries. Even today at
dinner parties someone invariably asks, 'What's a best boy?' Read this
book and find out!"

—ADAM HOLENDER, director of photography
(Midnight Cowboy, Smoke, Fresh)

"This book really 'hits the mark,' and if *you* want to as well, you need
to read it and find out how. It's very funny, perceptive, and most infor-
mative; it manages to cross those lines quite deftly."

—ANDREW DUNN, director of photography
(Sweet Home Alabama, Gosford Park, L.A. Story)

AN INSIDER'S GUIDE TO FILM SLANG

STRIKE THE BABY
and
KILL THE BLONDE

DAVE KNOX

THREE RIVERS PRESS • NEW YORK

Published in the United States by Three Rivers Press,
an imprint of the Crown Publishing Group, a division
of Random House, Inc., New York.

www.randomhouse.com

THREE RIVERS PRESS and the Tugboat design are
registered trademarks of Random House, Inc.

Printed in the United States of America

Design by Barbara M. Bachman

Library of Congress Cataloging-in-Publication Data

Knox, Dave.
    Strike the baby and kill the blonde: an insider's guide to
film slang / Dave Knox.—1st ed.
        1. Motion pictures—Dictionaries.   2. Cinematography—
Dictionaries.   I. Title.
    PN1993.45.K62 2005
    791.43'03—dc22   2004029033

ISBN 1-4000-9759-2

10 9 8 7 6 5 4 3 2 1

FIRST EDITION

FOR SARAH

ACKNOWLEDGMENTS

I'd like to thank all the people at Crown/Three Rivers Press, especially Orly Trieber, for publishing my book. My agent, Joanna Hurley, and the people at Hurley Media shepherded me all along the way. My friends Dave Whitford, Jim Meigs, and André Bernard offered encouragement and constructive criticism, while Pat Pruyne quickly solved all computer problems. My three "readers," Becca Mudge, Rob Crandall, and Sarah Knox, kept me on the right track, offering timely edits as well as suggestions for fine-tuning the book's humor. Many thanks. Having said that, any errors or misrepresentations are mine alone—I based the book totally on my own work experience, recollections, and attitudes.

INTRODUCTION

Go get me the two diving boards and the toilet seat for the camera dolly." This request came from the key grip (head rigging technician) on the set of the new Will Smith movie *Hitch* (aka *The Last First Kiss*), which we were filming in New York City, down in SoHo. Of course, I knew what George meant: He was going to affix extra platform space that would travel with the movie camera as I photographed the next shot. But to the layman? By using nicknames, he had identified specific equipment to the film crew and had disguised his meaning from passersby. Even a top-notch film student from New York University would have a hard time decoding his intentions. I began to think of all the confusing slang used every day on the movie set.

"Go fetch me a show card!" Fresh from college (where I received the aptly named B.S. in Speech from Northwestern University), on my first day on a real movie set, I didn't understand what was being asked of me. Well, my first day on a television commercial set, that is. In the past, I had supported myself as a commercial still photographer, and I'd graduated from a premier film program, but this one was new to me. "What is it, your first day?" Actually, yes. How was I to know that a simple two-by-three-foot black-and-white piece of cheap cardboard was one of the primary tools of the professional filmmaker?

The director and cameraman of that Crisco commercial, Elbert Budin, strode past the line of cooked chicken pieces, over a thousand in all. "That one, that one there, *not* that one." He was auditioning chicken pieces, all precooked and laid out on tabletops for the commercial spot. The assistant cameraperson rigged Elbert's German-made movie camera for slow-motion filming, and the end of the day found me catching flying chicken pieces with my show card. We simply tossed the individual pieces of chicken into the air, and Elbert filmed them in slow motion on the way down, to demonstrate the idea that chicken cooked in Crisco was . . . lighter than air. I was hooked.

From there, it was a matter of gaining the technical skills with the camera equipment that would allow me to graduate from the ranks of chicken wrangler. I spent a year managing a film stage in Lower Manhattan, where I handled everything from painting sets to repairing lighting gear to walking the vicious guard dog. I was enamored of the large complicated movie cameras that came through the stage. Mitchell, Arriflex, Panavision . . . To me, these names meant HOLLY-WOOD. Using my passkey on weekends, I was able to sneak back onto the stage and rifle through cases of expensive camera gear. With no one else around except for the trusty dog, El Capitán, I taught myself the technical intricacies of the different motion-picture camera systems. In the 1960s, the great German director Werner Herzog reportedly stole the camera he needed to make his first film, so my extracurricular activities put me in good company. The next year when the time came to take the test for admission to the union as assistant cameraperson, I passed with flying colors.

I worked as camera assistant on several films over the next two years, including manning an extra camera on the cult classic *The Toxic Avenger,* but once again something new and wonderful caught my eye. A screening of Francis Coppola's *One from the Heart* left me breathless. How did they photograph all those beautiful, intricate moving-camera shots? I had never seen anything like it. The Steadicam had been invented by Garrett Brown in 1973, and used on such high-profile films as *Rocky* and *Saturday Night Fever,* but was still seen by the industry as something rare and exotic. I contacted Brown and took one of the first weeklong training classes for camera operators dedicated to the Steadicam, a mobile camera system worn strapped to the operator's body. Everything about the Steadicam appealed to me. It addressed all my interests—camerawork, choreography, precision, athletics. I borrowed some money and bought a beat-up Steadicam rig from the manufacturer, Cinema Products, practicing camera moves alone in my apartment with imaginary actors for months. A phone call: Garrett Brown had recommended me for a job on a feature film shooting in Pennsylvania. Was I ready?

We were lined up to begin filming on *Maria's Lovers,* my first major Hollywood film as a camera operator. I was twenty-five years old and had grown a bushy red beard in an attempt to look a little older. Hopefully I could convince my coworkers that I was an experienced hand at this moviemaking stuff. The actors Nastassja Kinski and John Savage were in front of me, and I was standing next to the director with the Steadicam strapped to my back. The Russian director Andrei Konchalovsky wrapped a porcelain plate into a napkin. Suddenly he brought his foot down hard. *Crash!* The plate was smashed for good luck; filming could begin. I'm not sure how his film fared at the box office, but my career as a Steadicam and camera operator on Hollywood films was taking off.

The director may tell the actors what to do, but the cinematographer (or director of photography—DP) designs the shots that make up the film, and the camera operator is the DP's right hand. It's the camera operator who stands closest to the actors during a scene, standing, in fact, between the director and his actors. The operator holds the camera and crafts the shots that describe the director's vision; the film is literally in my hands at that moment. My eye gazes through the eyepiece as the action unfolds. If you think about it, I see the movie first. It sometimes takes screenwriters, directors, and producers years to bring their films to the screen. Endless months of meetings, planning sessions, location scouting, and casting. The camera crew, however, is hired for only the brief (four- to twenty-week) exciting period of time called principal photography. This is the most rewarding part of moviemaking, where set design, photography, and acting all come together, and something new and wonderful is conjured out of thin air. Sometimes, when staring at a scene through the eyepiece, you just *know* something special is unfolding. Watching Al Pacino do something unpredictable, new, and astonishing on take number ten after a long day of shooting on *City Hall,* or setting up a stunt where the actors Joaquin Phoenix and Vince Vaughan ride a bike down a steep jungle hillside on location in Thailand for *Return to Paradise*—these are just two of the indelible memories I have from the set.

Now, twenty years and over one hundred films later, it's hard not to be a bit nostalgic as I review some of the highlights. Early in my career, I was more of a specialist. Moving-camera techniques, with the audience as a participant in the scene, were becoming more and more popular with directors. Sometimes I landed on a film crew for a week, or even just for a day, to lend a hand with special sequences. I flew into North Carolina and joined the crew of *Dirty Dancing* just long enough to shoot two key sequences with my Steadicam and to attend the wrap party. I worked the first week on *The Silence of the Lambs,* contributing the moving camera to the opening credits, chasing Jodie Foster as she ran through the training course at FBI headquarters in Quantico, Virginia. On the set of *Black Rain,* I followed Michael Douglas chasing bad guys through a meat market in lower New York and received a swinging slab of beef to the head for my efforts. I've been the man behind the camera and had an opportunity to meet many of America's favorite stars, such as Meryl Streep, Robin

Williams, Sylvester Stallone, Robert De Niro, and Adam Sandler. Or perhaps you're a fan of the younger actresses Winona Ryder, Julia Stiles, Kirsten Dunst, and Christina Ricci? Well, I met and photographed them all early in their careers, when they were finding their way as young performers, before they were famous stars.

Looking back on that first day shooting a Crisco commercial, I couldn't have predicted where the movie business would take me: from Ireland on *Devil's Own* to China and Thailand on *Return to Paradise,* literally from Hollywood to Hoboken. I've been fortunate to be given an opportunity to practice my craft in a job I love, in an industry populated by interesting and glamorous individuals.

Now, to return to the toilet seat and diving board story . . . wouldn't you like to know what all those movie people are talking about? Everyone enjoys watching movies, but what exactly is a workday like on the set of a major motion picture? What really goes on behind the scenes? If you've ever sat through the closing credits and thought, "What the heck is a best boy?" this is the book for you. Perhaps you're a student and are thinking about trying to become a Hollywood actor or director. Then again, maybe you just want to sound like a movie-industry professional and amaze your friends with insider information. *Strike the Baby and Kill the Blonde* is organized along the lines of a dictionary to help you find explanations for specific film terms (and to settle bets during friendly discussions). On the other hand, readers looking for an immersion experience in the world of Hollywood filmmaking can choose to read it from cover to cover. It will provide you with an entertaining read, as well as a glimpse at the workings of the movie cast and crew in action. The language of Hollywood moviemaking has always been top secret, until now. I hope you enjoy the book—now, pass me a showcard.

A camera: When more than one movie camera is being used on set, the camera **crew** very cleverly designates them *A, B, C,* and so forth, so that praise or blame can be properly attributed to the crew after viewing the **dailies.**

Abby Singer: The next-to-last **shot** to be photographed by the **crew** on a particular day is universally referred to by movie **crews** as the Abby, though no one knows exactly why. I have heard that Mr. Singer was employed at one time as an **AD,** but it's curious that his name has become synonymous with the *second*-to-last shot. Maybe his crews filmed only two shots a day?

above the line: Refers to highly paid movie personnel, including **producers, writers, directors,** and **actors.** Their salaries are part of the above-the-line costs of filmmaking, and are accounted for separately by **studio** accountants from the rest of the daily filmmaking expenses. Did you know that **crew** people are paid weekly, but movie **stars** usually receive all their salary before the **cameras** roll?

AC: (1) Assistant cameraperson. See also **focus puller, loader.** This key **crew** position is the person responsible for the care and feeding of the highly technical (and expensive) motion-picture **camera** equipment. The job includes anything that might aid the **DP** (**cinematographer**) in capturing the images, from physically moving the camera to cleaning the **lenses**. Most films employ two to six people in this capacity.

(2) Alternating current—the kind of electricity you get from the plug on the wall (in the USA, 120 volts AC).

Academy: A couple of thousand **actors**, sound **mixers**, **directors**, camerapeople . . . a cross-section of film-industry workers make up the membership of the Academy of Motion Picture Arts and Sciences and vote on the **Oscars**. Sometime just before the awards ceremony, their mailboxes become clogged with free videos, DVDs, **soundtrack** CDs, fruit baskets, bundles of cash . . . all sent by **producers** hoping to receive votes for their pet projects.

Academy Award: Oscar, baby! The ultimate statue for the mantelpiece. Well, there is the Nobel Peace Prize—but I hear the competition is pretty fierce, and it's probably *who* you know, anyway.

academy leader: Remember the 16-millimeter (16mm) films you may have seen in school? The film showing started with a countdown (ten, nine, eight . . .) and a sweeping second hand. That's the official academy leader (strip of film) that is edited onto the beginning of most films shot B.D. (before digital). The academy leader helps the **projectionist** line up the picture properly on the screen and prefocus the film.

acetate base: Also called safety base, the clear tough strip of film to which the **emulsion** of light-sensitive silver particles is attached. At some point during the 1940s, **projectionists** noticed a slight problem with movie film: It kept bursting into flames! No kidding. Around 1950, all **nitrate** base **film stock** was outlawed and quickly replaced by the new acetate base, though many old films from pre–World War II were never reprinted, and hundreds have been lost forever.

action: (1) The command that cues **actors** to start acting, always spoken *only* by the **director**. The words used to initiate the entire filming sequence are **"roll sound,"** said by the **AD**. And no one ever says, "Lights, camera, action!" That's an archaic phrase from early **Hollywood**. The old **arc** lights then in use needed a little extra time to warm up.

(2) *Action* can also describe the physical aspects of the intended **shot**, as in "De Niro's action . . . He runs through the alley and dives under that parked car." During a **stunt** sequence, the director will cede control for safety reasons, and the **stunt coordinator** is the one who calls, "Action!"

actor: The man on screen doing the talking. Can be a **leading man**, a **baddie**, a character actor, or, on a sitcom TV **show**, the "wacky neighbor." Hey, did I miss something, or are actresses suddenly now all referring to themselves as actors instead of **actresses** in the media? No problem, happy to make the change, but it wasn't on the **call sheet**.

actress: See **actor**—only . . . female. These can take the form of ingenue, leading lady, or grandma. Regrettably, there are few roles for lovely, experienced, middle-aged women in **Hollywood** films. Actresses can either try to stay young looking for as long as possible (see **diffusion**), or wait until they've reached grandma age and attempt a comeback.

AD: Assistant director. You might think the assistant director is primarily a creative job, helping the **director** to bring his or her artistic vision to the screen. However, the job is not a "junior director," as the name insinuates. On the set, an AD is like a communications officer or army general. ADs command a staff of **PAs**. They coordinate all the **actors**, work with the **DP** to schedule the day's work, and answer a million questions. Where is the next **location**? Where can we get fifty monkeys by tomorrow for the *Temple of Doom* scene? When the hell are we going to break for lunch? The AD has the answer.

additional pages: Last-minute script **rewrites** are printed on colored paper, to make sense of the many changes, and the pages are numbered to track down anyone leaking the **plot** to their pals via the Internet. By the end of the **shoot**, an up-to-date **script** ends up resembling a rainbow-printed mess.

ad-lib: When **actors** take it upon themselves to nullify the best efforts of the writer, **producer**, and **director** and *make up their own dialogue*! Yes! I know some moviegoers out there think that Stallone and Schwarzenegger themselves think up all those witty sayings, but trust me, everything's in the **screenplay**. Sorry, I hope you're not disappointed, but there are simply very few actors who can say it better than the **screenwriter**. Having said that, comic geniuses like Mike Myers, Eddie Murphy, and Robin Williams are given pretty much a free hand to ad-lib.

ADR: Automated dialog replacement. Also termed *looping*. The **actors** watch the completed scenes in an L.A. **editing** suite months after **principal photography** has ended, and then attempt to re-record their voices. This is to replace a flawed original recording of the **dialogue**. The finished visuals play in a continuous loop, so the actors can have many tries at matching the lip movements and vocal delivery of the original scene. There's a great scene between Meryl Streep and Gene Hackman in the movie *Postcards from the Edge* that shows the mechanics of looping quite well.

advance schedule: Next week's or next month's work is listed on the advance schedule for that particular film. Each **department** on the film (sound, **props, camera,** and the like) can consult it as an aid in planning big-ticket rental items, such as cars, **cranes,** and **extras.**

aerials: Shots filmed from airplanes, helicopters, or hot air balloons, often by a specialized **2nd unit**. You can't steer a balloon, and airplanes generally whiz by too fast for controlled photography, so most aerials for movies are filmed from helicopters. These are expensive to rent (five hundred dollars per hour) and have an annoying tendency to crash at inopportune moments. The late Vic Morrow was one fine actor who met his untimely end via whirling helicopter blades while filming John Landis's *Twilight Zone: The Movie.*

agent: Movie **stars** have agents who work on landing jobs, negotiating more money, and securing better conditions, but the **producers, directors, DPs, writers,** and **art directors** may be represented by agents, as well. This has created a veritable subculture in L.A. of well-dressed people wining and dining each other, all promoting their various interests and maneuvering around in an attempt to place their clients on the A-list projects. Have your people call my people!

Alan Smithee: This is the fake name adopted in the **credits** by **directors** when, for whatever reason, the finished film doesn't meet their lofty standards. (Excuse me, but weren't they in charge on the set?) After a lot of name-calling during **postproduction,** and fighting among director, **producer,** and **writer,** the director will get fed up and remove his or her name from the film, using the name Alan Smithee instead. Once you start looking around, you'll see the name everywhere. . . . Alan Smithee made a *lot* of films.

ambience: See **room tone.**

anamorphic: Top-secret **camera** geek word meaning "wide screen." Anamorphic **lenses** compress the horizontal picture element in a ratio of 2 to 1, allowing a standard movie camera, with a square-shaped imaging area, to photograph a wider, panoramic shot. Ever see real skinny cowboys over the credits at the beginning and end of a **John Ford** cowboy film? That's because the original film was shot with anamorphic lenses and now they're trying to fit all the **wide-screen** information (such as titles) into your little TV box at home. See also **aspect ratio, pan and scan.**

animation: Cartoons. Technically speaking, anything from film scratches and sock puppets in an **art film** to clay figures (like Gumby) to Bugs Bunny are all animations. Computers are used today to generate images without the help of **actors** whatsoever. (We really need only their voices for the **soundtrack.**) A modern well-executed animated film like *Toy Story* or *Finding Nemo* can make you forget you're watching a download off someone's computer hard drive and can describe a wonderful imaginary world. In the wake of all this progress, the great films of Nick Park (Wallace & Gromit) have revived the old retro Claymation techniques.

animation cel: Once upon a time, individual pictures were laboriously hand-drawn by scores of artists and carefully photographed in an exact sequence to produce cel animation, such as Bugs Bunny.

The individual pictures are called cels because they are drawn onto large sheets of clear celluloid.

animation stand: When cartoons are made from **animation cels**, they're photographed by a huge **camera** mounted to the wall and suspended looking straight down from six feet overhead. The **animator** places the cel to be photographed on a table at waist height and clicks a button, similar to a modern computer mouse, to take an individual picture, before repeating the whole process with the next cel. It is unbelievably time consuming, as it takes twenty-four pictures to make *one second* of film. One slip of the hand can set you back days. In the early 1980s, when I worked as an animator at Darino Films, I had a very productive morning, finishing a whole stack of cels. Ready for a break, I erased my entire morning's work when I misfired the mouse/clicker while reaching for a coffee cup. Ouch!

animator: Person drawing cartoons. In today's world, it's probably more accurate to say "person sitting alone, playing with a computer."

animatronic: This word is a synonym for *robotic.* You know, not human, like the acting in the recent films of George Lucas.

answer printing: See **timing**.

aperture: The blades of the aperture ring **(iris)** inside the **camera lens** control how much light reaches the film, and the aperture is the size of the hole, generally rated in **f-stops** or **t-stops**. Further, these have cryptic numerical designations such as 2.8 or 5.6, and apart from providing the **crew** with some practice with elementary mathematics, these numbers affect everything from the lightness or darkness of the photographed scene to the potential sharpness of the

focus. For this reason, the setting of the aperture is the sole domain of the most important **crew** member, the director of photography (**DP**).

apple: (1) When the **camera** changes angle slightly between **shots**, the next **take** is labeled take 1A, and verbally called out as "take one, apple," in an attempt to avoid confusion. Every take filmed during the movie needs a unique number-and-letter combo to aid the **editor** in finding the good stuff in the midst of all the **false starts, no prints,** and **pickups.**

(2) Apple (Macintosh) is also the brand of computer favored by creative film-industry types, hands down.

apple box: A small black plywood box (12 x 8 x 20 inches), literally and figuratively one of the building blocks of filmmaking. Apples, or the smaller **half-apples,** and **pancakes** are used every day to raise and lower furniture, **props, dolly track,** and even **actors.** When two actors are in a single **shot,** and they differ dramatically in height, sometimes the smaller one will be asked to do the shot standing on an apple box. Of course, one must be diplomatic when asking a movie **star** to stand on what is commonly referred to as a **man-maker.**

arc: An arc is a very large DC (direct current, like in batteries) **movie light.** So named because the arc (spark) between two contacts makes the light, with no metal filament, as you might find in a regular lightbulb. Because one extra technician per lighting unit is required to continually adjust the internal contacts, the more economical **HMI** light has replaced the venerable arc. Another **Hollywood** tradition completely down the drain.

Arri: The Arriflex Motion Picture Camera Company takes its name from *Arnold* and *Richter,* who developed the first reflex-viewing (what you see is what you get) **cameras** for Germany during World

War II. Arri is still making high-quality cameras in Austria and Germany, and more movies have been **shot** with Arris than with any other camera. The quality of the Arri design is clearly demonstrated by the World War II footage filmed by the German forces with their Arris, which far surpasses the footage shot by the Americans with their unwieldy **Mitchell** or Bell & Howell cameras. You can view this footage twenty-four hours a day on cable TV on the History Channel: "All Nazis—All the Time!"

art department: Without the art department, moviemakers would have no background against which to photograph the **stars.** They provide all the scenery, furniture, **props,** and pretty much everything that doesn't move in front of the **camera.** Even low-budget films need some help from the art department, to dress up a **found location.** You might be able to talk **actors** into working on your low-budget student film for free, but please set aside some **money** for the art department. And **craft service.**

art director: Works with, and just under, the overall **production designer** to create the environment for filming—the **set.** Often seen passing around hand-drawn sketches and swatches of fabric, the art director contributes greatly to the "look" of the film. Weeks before filming begins, the art director has drawn the sets and then overseen their construction on a **soundstage.** Last-minute flashes of inspiration and changes by the **director** hopefully can be limited to the **actors** and the **dialogue,** as **art department** changes usually entail rebuilding and refurnishing large spaces.

art film: This is a film that will never play at the cineplex. In fact, the only people who might be found screening art films are masochistic movie critics and film students who are forced to watch

CRITIC'S
CHOICE

them by well-meaning professors. A good example is Andy Warhol's film *Empire,* an eight-hour single-shot film of New York's Empire State Building. Watch out for a stampede as you head for the exits!

ASA: These letters stand for American Standards Association. The speed rating (sensitivity of the film's **emulsion** to light) of film is measured in numbers such as 100 ASA, 400 ASA, and so on. Even today's little digital point-and-shoot **cameras** use these numbers to quantify their response to light levels. This rating is one of the variables in determining **exposure** and tells you the amount of light (either sunlight or the artificial kind) you need in order to successfully make a **shot**. Some time around 1990, the letters ISO staged a coup d'etat and took over from the letters ASA, and consequently film is now rated 100 ISO, 400 ISO, etc. No one seems to have noticed.

ASC: Ever wonder what those letters after the names in the **credits** designate? Everybody knows what M.D. and D.D.S. stand for, but what the hell is ASC? It means the person in question is a member of an exclusive club, the American Society of Cinematographers. One needs to have photographed five **feature** films and be sponsored by a member to join. Canadian **camera** folks have the CSC, Brits have the BSC, Aussies have the ACS. (They do things backwards down there.) **Editors** have the ACE.

aside: More of a convention on the Broadway stage than in the movies, an aside is when **actors** turn away and talk to themselves. In everyday life, this is considered rude, or perhaps crazy. Another name for this in the movies is a **throwaway line**. An actor will speak the line under his or her breath, and often this has the effect of "drawing in" the audience and making the words seem more personal.

aspect ratio: Here's another example of a fairly complicated math term that is understood by virtually everyone involved in the movie business, from the **PA** to the **producer,** and yet has remained a secret to the layman. Ready? Take a deep breath. The ratio of the movie or TV screen width to its height is called the aspect ratio. Forget about Sony's marketing measurements like "thirty-four-inch diagonal screen"—chances are your TV set is shaped in the ratio of 4:3, width to height. Regular American feature films are photographed in 1.85:1 (16:9), giving an image slightly wider than the average TV. In order for these to be shown on a smaller home TV screen, they're reformatted in a process called **pan and scan** and relabeled **full screen** version.

assistant cameraperson: The **camera operator's** right hand. See **AC, focus puller.**

assistant director: See **AD.** He or she (along with the **DP**) translates the **director's** flights of fancy into **shooting schedules** and concrete **shots.**

assistant to the director: This is quite different from **assistant director (AD).** The assistant director is the on-set general, amassing the material and troops to fight the enemy . . . I mean shoot the film. The assistant *to* the director is a low-level **production assistant** who follows the boss around, making sure a cup of Starbucks coffee is always close at hand, the laundry gets picked up, and the cell phone batteries are fully charged. They do all the stuff for the **director** that most normal people are forced to do for themselves. This is why directors prefer to drag movie shoots on for weeks, often until the **producer** is forced to **pull the plug.** Of course, producers and **stars** are also assigned one personal assistant each for the **run of the film.**

associate producer: This "almost a producer" job title, just above **production manager** in the hierarchy, is sometimes given as a perk to a helpful person (**writer, AD,** girlfriend, or some combination thereof) who has proved worthy during the filming.

audition: Trying out for an acting part on movies generally takes the form of reading through some **sides** (two to three pages of the

script) in front of the **director** and perhaps a **producer**. Sometimes the sessions are videotaped to keep track of the many **actors** and **actresses** who are under consideration, but the old **Hollywood** "screen test" in front of a whole movie **crew**, with lights and **cameras**, is a thing of the past. Too expensive. Also, today's big **stars** never "read for a part." Rather, they land job offers through an informal network of breakfast or lunch meetings between **producers** and **agents** on the West Coast.

auteur theory: This phrase never comes up on a working movie **set,** but in case you are a student and want to skip **film school,** I'll explain. French film critics in the 1950s and 1960s, centered on the magazine *Cahiers du cinema,* started studying a **director's** entire body of work and drawing conclusions about the person based on their findings. For instance, Spielberg . . . likes aliens but is afraid of sharks . . . something like that.

auto-focus: One big difference between the professional cameraperson and Dad with the home video is that the pro wouldn't be caught dead using auto-focus. In fact, on a $200,000 **Panavision** movie **camera,** there is no electronic or mechanical auto-focus system, something found on every cheap Japanese home video camera. Focusing is the exclusive domain of a single person, the **focus puller.** For better-looking home videos and iMovies, my number one helpful hint is *turn off the bloody auto-focus!* You can easily turn the focus knob at the end of the lens yourself. Try it, and amaze your friends. Your videos will look a lot better. Trust me.

availability: When **producers** call a **freelance crew** person or **actor** on the phone, they generally want to know two things: your availability (are you free for the days, weeks, or months in question) and your **rate.** Your potential interest in the project in question is usually taken for granted. (Why wouldn't you jump at the chance to work on *That Darn Cat: The Early Years*?)

available light: This means that cumbersome **gennys, trucks,** and large **movie lights** are unnecessary, as the intended **scene** will be photographed using only daylight, or at night, with the light provided by streetlights and storefronts. (See **Dogma.**) In theory, one can shoot a whole **feature** film using only available light, but often "reality" needs a little help from the **gaffer.**

Avid: Digital **editing** equipment that single-handedly put the old-time Moviola editing gear out to pasture. No more need to "cut" the film. You feed all the information into the Avid computer, and with the touch of a button you can do all kinds of cool **special effects** and regular old editing, as well. Apple Computer's **Final Cut Pro** is another digital editing system, favored by filmmakers on a tighter budget.

Avid-gazing: This recent term refers to **directors'** tendencies to fall in love with their films during **editing.** In the past, directors would take a well-earned and much-needed vacation upon conclusion of **principal photography,** while the **editor** laboriously hacked out a **rough cut.** Now it's easy to push a few computer buttons and just watch your marvelous movie creation for hours on end! As a result, finished films end up being longer these days, as directors become enraptured of the footage they've worked so hard to photograph. Movies all used to be ninety minutes long—what happened?

B camera: When using **multicamera** techniques on a film, the additional **camera** and the **crew** using it are called the B camera. For instance, I manned the B camera on *Scent of a Woman* and like to think in some small way I share in the **Oscar** Al Pacino won for his role as Frank Slade. I'm not sure if Al sees it the same way. . . . When a third angle is needed for photographing a **stunt** or other unrepeatable action, the camera and crew are called—you got it— C camera. If shooting in a **studio** with video cameras, in a flash of creativity, they are often designated 1, 2, 3 instead. B camera is not to be confused with the network video term **B roll**. On a feature film, the B camera works alongside the A camera, photographing a different angle of the same **scene**.

B roll: This is a term, used in video and TV production only (not **features**), that designates additional **cutaway shots** and other generic footage the **editor** might later need to shape the story. On feature films, this is the rough equivalent of shooting **second unit**.

baby: This is a 750- or 1,000-watt movie light with a squiggly shaped **fresnel** lens on the front. Something you rarely hear at the supermarket, but every day on a movie set: **"Strike the baby!"** (Take the small lamp away!)

baby legs: This is a short aluminum a̶ tripod, used for making **shots** between tw̶ ground. Back when these were made of̶ used to be a bit taller and were termed s̶ low shots at ground level, use a **hi hat**.

back end: This is money distributed to select, very clever people (**producers** and **actors** mostly) from percentages of profits generated by a film after all the expenses of filming and distribution are accounted for. Sometimes an offer is made to **crew** and **cast** to work on a film for **scale**, with a back-end deal to make up for the lack of actual **money**. Presumably after producers' expenses are recouped, and the movie is a hit, the back-end money is paid out. Profits are often disguised by creative **Hollywood** accounting, so watch your back end.

back to one: This is the phrase the **assistant director** uses to reset the **background actors** (nonspeaking **extras**) to their beginning places. Since films are generally made by piecing together **shots** taken with only one **camera** but filmed at different times, the extras need to be coached to repeat their movements on each take, matching **actions** exactly. Not an easy task.

background (BG): Just what you think: things in a **scene** not given prominence. Also refers to the nonspeaking **actors**, hired by the dozen (**dayplayers**) and sent over by the **casting agent** and who are coached by the **AD**. During filming, the players of the background are coached to **mime** talking. They try to stay as quiet as possible, and the **sound department** focuses on recording the utterances of only the highly paid principal **talent**. The chatter of guests and the crashing of dropped dinner plates are added later during **postproduction**. It's actually quite entertaining to witness a completely me being filmed. I did some work on *The Age of Innocence*, whole ballroom filled with silent dancing Victorians in full costume was quite a sight.

background action: This is called out loudly by the **AD** after **"roll sound"** and just before the director calls **"Action!"** to jump-start the **extras** prior to cueing the principal **talent**.

backlight: Kodak's instructional literature for years stated, "Put the sun at your back when filming." Wrong! What you want to do is arrange a **scene** so that the sun or a large light source is behind the **actor**. This gives the subject's hair a heavenly glow and helps make everyone, from beautiful movie **actresses** to your mother-in-law, look better.

backlot: Extra space outdoors owned by a big movie **studio** (Warner Bros., FOX, Universal), which is dedicated to welcoming tourists and providing **ridefilms** and which can also be occasionally used for filming. All the conveniences are nearby (lights, **cameras**, commissary) and none of the hassle or expense of traveling with the **crew** to Rome, Paris, or New York. Just put up some building **facades** on the backlot, and presto! You're in the Bronx! One potential problem is that films made on a backlot, such as *Singin' in the Rain* or *West Side Story*, tend to look as though they were, well, shot on a backlot.

baddie or **bad guy:** A **director** might describe a **scene** by saying, "In this **shot**, the **hero** comes around the corner, chased by two baddies." An actor might evolve over the years from a **leading man** to a character actor to a baddie—look at Gary Busey.

ballast: Today's huge movie lights need a big heavy boxy contraption, called the *ballast,* attached between the power source and the lamp head. The ballast stores up a lot of current, and "striking" the ballast means to fire it up, rather than the usual meaning for "striking," which is to take something away. Let's review: To strike something from the **set** means to take it away, unless "it" is a ballast—and then it means to restart it. Got it?

banana: When the **director** wants the **actor** to walk across the set in an arc, instead of a straight line (this may look more natural when interpreted by the **lens**), he asks them to banana. One of the many skills required of movie actors (in addition to learning the lines) is to move in particular ways for the camera, and the banana into and out of camera view is a cornerstone of movie acting. Once you've mastered it, move on to the **Hollywood stand-up**.

barndoor: Metal flaps on the outside of movie lights that can be adjusted to shape the light beam. Other items used to shape the light (or to actually create shadows) are **eggcrates, flags,** and **teasers**.

barney: A formfitting foam-and-cloth sweater can be zipped over the **mag** when a movie **camera** is making too much noise (due to design, maintenance problems, or questionable **raw stock**) for shooting on a quiet interior **soundstage**. This extra layer of padding can help keep the camera warm, as well. The term is derived from Barney Google's horse blanket, for you readers of old-time comic books.

base camp: A movie **crew** is anywhere from 20 to 150 people, and it travels around like an army, commandeering civic locations for its own purposes and parking indiscriminately. Base camp houses the cars, trucks, extra equipment, makeup trailer, and **catering** tent. Just a little farther up the street, you'll find the **set**.

basher: East Coast slang for an **eyelight**. See **obie**. A little **camera**-mounted frontlight can certainly add a little sparkle to the **actor** or **actress's** eyes.

batteries: Since we all use computers and cell phones, everyone is becoming familiar with ni-cads, lithiums, and other sophisticated rechargeable batteries. Just imagine how big, powerful, expensive, and heavy such a battery must be to run a huge movie **camera**. It's the size of a lunch box, puts out 35 amps/hour, costs thousands, and weighs sixty pounds. One of these could power your laptop for years, but it would certainly cut down on its portability.

baylight: A homemade overhead light fixture, sometimes called a softbox, or box light. Popularized by the **DP** Gordon Willis during the shooting of *The Godfather,* the baylight creates soft, natural, light streaming down from above. This was a break from traditional **Hollywood** glamour lighting, and helped create a moody setting for the Corleone family.

bazooka: This is a large metal monopod, which assembles in sections to provide a support base for a big movie **camera**. Its chief advantage over a conventional **tripod** is that it is easier to fit into tight places. And it has a much cooler name. It looks just like an army bazooka.

b-board: Big thick pieces of Styrofoam are sometimes used to re-flect light onto a **scene**, called bounce board, or b-board. Standard size is four feet by eight feet, and smaller chunks can be cut as needed. (Grips carry knives!) See **Phil Collins**.

beat: Very common **on-set** phrase, this is **actor**-speak for a pe-riod of time, generally described by other people as one second. The

director might instruct, "Wait a beat, and then run into the room firing a pistol! **Action!**"

bee smoke: Used by apiarists to calm swarms of nasty stinging creatures, bee smoke, dispersed into the air from a tin can, is occasionally used as atmospheric **smoke** on movies. Sometimes it has a calming effect on the **crew's** intestines, as well, causing a run on the **honeywagon**.

beefy baby: A beefy baby is a small, heavy-duty lighting stand, which is used as a complement to a **pigeon**, a **low-boy**, or a preemie baby. I'm not makin' this stuff up!

below the line: The term used to describe all movie **crew** personnel, from the godlike **DP** down to the lowly **PAs**. Their salaries and all the equipment rentals, **costume** purchases, set construction costs, and so forth are categorized as below-the-line costs. These expenses haven't changed much over the years, when corrected for inflation. The high cost of making movies, which has been widely reported in the media, can be traced to **above-the-line** costs, that is, **screenwriter**, **director**, and **star** salaries.

best boy: No, not the director's pet. In the **crew** hierarchy, the best boy is the 2nd electrician, working under the **gaffer**. Sometimes there is also a best boy **grip**, working under the **key grip**. Are they indeed the *best*? Employee performance is such a subjective thing. . . .

big house: Not a prison, the big house to NYC film **crews** means Kaufman Astoria Studios in Queens, which has the largest indoor **soundstage** in the East. Many famous films and TV shows have been filmed there, from the Marx Brothers classic *A Night at the Opera* to *The Cosby Show*.

bit player: Background **extra** who is given some special **business** or minor **dialogue**, and receives a title in the **credits** like Handsome Bartender or Gunman #3.

black and white: Before the advent of color in the 1940s, all films were photographed in black and white. Light focused through the camera **lens** struck a silver-coated light-sensitive **emulsion** inside a dark **camera body**, and there you have it! Movies! Or still photographs, anyway. It took New Jersey's own **Thomas Edison** to turn them into movies. Nowadays **directors** occasionally opt to shoot in black and white as an artistic choice, but may have difficulty selling their film, as producers and theater owners are often resistant. **Box office** numbers are generally higher for color projects.

blackout: In the world of Broadway theaahhter, this means the lights are turned out for dramatic effect at the end of a **scene**. In movies, this effect is achieved via a **fade-out**, created during **editing**. Most common of all in film is the straight cut, in which a new scene begins directly after the old scene, with no artsy fades or blackness at all.

blackwrap: Most movie lighting and **grip** equipment is colored black to reduce stray reflections, and aluminum foil is no exception. **Crews** use this black anodized metal foil to cover leaky lighting instruments, which otherwise spray light all over the set. See **flare**.

blimp: A balloon with a motor and a huge colorful corporate logo (Fuji, Goodyear), sometimes used for **aerials**, but this is only for live video, rarely for films.

In films, a blimp is the external metal housing that surrounded movie **cameras** from 1930 to 1960 in an attempt to make them quieter. Modern cameras are designed to be silent (self-blimped), though **crews** may sometimes resort to using a soft **barney** if requested by the sound **mixer**.

blocking: (1) The art of arranging **actors** within a scene, supervised by the **director** and **DP**. The actors' movements are choreographed, and the **shots** to be filmed are discussed. Tape **marks** may be placed on the floor during blocking to aid in planning. Blocking, lighting the set, then shooting are the three steps to getting an image onto film, and always in that order. Even low-budget **narrative** films adhere strictly to this formula.

(2) Another meaning of blocking is when one actor unintentionally leans into another actor's **close-up**, briefly obscuring the **camera's** view.

blocking rehearsal: Upon arrival at a new **location** or set, the **director** might ask to work alone with the **actors** for a few minutes. Why not—it's their movie. Following this **closed rehearsal** is the blocking rehearsal, in which the **thespians** perform the scripted scene for the key crew personnel (normally one or two people from each **department**). This aids each of them in planning their individual jobs. The **stand-ins** are ready to mimic the actors' body language, the **mixer** and **boom operator** plan how to achieve a good soundtrack, and the **DP**, aided by the **gaffer**, designs the lighting for the scene.

blonde: A blonde is slang for a 2,000-watt open-faced (no lens in front) quartz-bulb spotlight. Also termed a *mighty,* short for *mighty mole,* these will blow your house fuse if plugged into the wall directly. Better to plug it into a **genny** or use the smaller **redhead** instead. "Kill the blonde!" is of course a request to *turn off the spotlight.*

blue: Most common color for sheets of light-correction **gels,** blue is the opposite of **CTO** (orange). Blue gels come in full, half, and quarter grades. They're most often used on lights to shift the color of the resulting beam. (Think blue moonlight streaming into a bedroom.)

blue screen: Many **special effects** shots in movies from 1950 to 1990 were achieved by placing **actors** in front of plain bright blue backgrounds; the resulting footage is used as one layer in a multiple exposure. The solid blue background gave good separation between the picture elements, owing to movie film's extreme blue sensitivity. Somewhere along the way, blue screen technology got replaced by the **green screen,** which seems to work better with today's video and computer-based effects.

BNC: (1) **Mitchell cameras,** which dominated **Hollywood** filmmaking from 1940 to 1970, were designated blimped newsreel cameras, or BNC. I can't imagine chasing a breaking news story with a humongous (by today's standards) seventy-five-pound Mitchell **camera** in tow, and **Panavision** put them out of business permanently by eliminating the need for the noise-proofing **blimp** (an extra layer of heavy metal).

(2) *BNC* is also a video term that describes a type of twist-together plug (bayonet navy connector) used to carry a video or antenna signal. These are prone to frequent failure, so camera and video **crews** keep multiple **cables** on hand at all times. Having a problem with the picture on the **video assist**? It's a cable.

boards: (1) The camera **dolly** sometimes rides on pine planks (shelving boards), placed on the floor by the **dolly grip** in order to smooth out the ride. Not only the **camera operator**, but also the people viewing the film in the movie theater, will appreciate this. A plywood **dancefloor** can be used for the same purpose.

(2) Boards can be shorthand for **storyboards**. "Show me the boards for the flying monkey scene, C.B.!"

body double: Apparently, if the **shot** being planned calls for nudity and excludes the **star's** face, another **actor** or **actress** with a killer body is sometimes substituted, though I've never (in over a hundred movies) witnessed this. I mean, how many shots are just a close-up of a butt cheek or a leg or something? The **crew** is already there shooting the love **scene**; one can simply **pan** the camera over and film the star's leg. Contracts dictate how much of the leg you can show in the final film version, of course, but most actors are pretty comfortable in their own skins, if the crew shows a bit of sensitivity. See **closed set**.

body makeup: Skin tones for Caucasian actors are often smoothed and very slightly darkened with an application of makeup for movie photography. This helps hide any blemishes, freckles, or tattoos.

bogie: Also called a noncombatant. Movies borrow a lot of terminology from the military and police forces. In the air force, a bogie is an enemy plane flying overhead, and on the movie **set**, a bogie is a person not affiliated with the **production** who dares to walk near the camera during filming. If the **lens** catches them staring, they're termed **lookie-loos**. They are politely asked to "move along" by the crack team of **PAs**.

Bollywood: Quick, which country produces the most movies? Wrong! It's India. Did you know over eight hundred 35 mm motion-picture films are photographed and shown in theaters each year in India? The Bollywood film industry is centered in Bombay (Mumbai). *Bollywood* is also a term describing the particular style of extravagant singing, dancing, and fighting films produced there.

bomb: A film that has failed to live up to the optimistic financial expectations of the producers and the **studio**, that is, a **turkey**.

bond company: Before any potential film can get financing, a promise (bond) is issued by a corporate insurance entity (the bond company) agreeing to cover any potential production cost overruns. In practice, when a **producer** uses up all the initial money provided in the budget, the bond company steps in. They supply the needed extra **money**, and will get their money back from the first profits. In many cases, the bond company remains in the background, happy to let the overbudget production carry on unchanged. Sometimes however, they descend on the set, hire or fire anybody who suits them (including the **director**), revamp the remaining **shooting schedule**, and even tell the **crew** exactly what shots to do. Hey, it's the movie *business.*

bonded lot: A well-lit, well-guarded, fully insured facility that parks large trucks overnight—which just might happen to be filled with valuables such as **props**, sound gear, and movie **cameras**.

boom: (1) *Boom* is a verb meaning "to raise the **camera** during a **shot**." Think about the ending shot in *Casablanca*. Humphrey Bogart and Claude Rains stroll away arm in arm as the camera rises up, up, up, and the **credits** roll. That's a boom up.

(2) Another meaning for *boom* is the actual moving part of the **dolly** or **crane** that the **dolly grip** manipulates in order to raise or lower the camera. This is different from a **tilt**, which is executed by

the **camera operator** at the **camera head**. Keep away from this part of the dolly if you value your fingers and toes. I've seen a hydraulic boom lose power and send the camera people, the lens, and a seventy-pound **Panavision** camera to the ground in a big pile in less than a second. Bring out the **B camera**!

boom operator: The second person in the **sound department**. He or she works under the **mixer** and is generally found performing a sort of dancing joust with the **camera operator**, waving the **boom pole** around, and aiming for a good **mic** placement whilst keeping this gear just clear of the **shot**. Look for the small black blob dancing above the actors next time you view a movie of the week (**MOW**).

boom pole: Sometimes called a fishpole. These expensive, long, lightweight, high-tech, telescoping carbon-fiber devices hold the sound **mic**. In a pinch, those cheap wooden paint roller extensions ($7.95) from the hardware store will work fine.

boom shadow: Items placed between movie lights and **actors** will cast ugly shadows during filming, and are very unpopular with the **DP** and the **director**. When the shadow looks like a **mic** on a **boom pole**, everyone knows whom to blame, the **boom operator**. Two solutions for a boom shadow are (1) a proper **rehearsal** for cast and crew—this way the **camera operator** and the boom operator can coordinate their movements—and (2) the addition of a **topper** (flag) to the lamp casting the shadow (if the DP agrees).

bounce: When light is redirected onto the scene by shining the lamp into the ceiling or a white **showcard**, it's called a bounce. Soft, nearly shadowless lighting is the result, a great alternative to harsh direct sunlight. Just don't bounce the intensely hot film or video lights directly at a safety sprinkler head or a valuable oil painting.

(As **DP**, I've done both. Not good. The first resulted in a visit by eager ax-wielding firemen, the other in a melted, gooey canvas.)

box office: (1) The place you go to buy the tickets at the Broadway theater, or better, the cineplex.

(2) Box office also refers to the amount of money earned by a film in **theatrical distribution**. See also **weekend**.

break a leg: This is what one says in the **green room** before a show to encourage an **actor** debuting on the Broadway stage, instead of "Good luck!" Never under any circumstances say "Good luck!" to a serious actor. He or she will not be pleased.

breakaway: Any **prop** or **set piece** designed to crumble, crush, or break on impact during filming. When preparing the **set**, colored **tape** warns people away from expensive breakable **props** intended for the actor's use. I'd love to throw an Old West party, where all the chairs are balsa wood, and beer bottles are lightweight **sugar glass**. When the party gets rowdy, simply smash a chair or a bottle over someone's head!

breakdown: This is what the **producer** has when the film goes over budget and the **bond company** is called. Alternatively, a breakdown is a comprehensive detailed list made from a close reading of the **script**. A breakdown lists all items and tasks of a similar nature, such as small hand **props**, particular days a certain actor works, or the days a **crane** rental might be needed.

breakfast burrito: Often the **producer** will provide a hot breakfast to start the day and to jump-start the **crew**, and a breakfast burrito (eggs, veggies, salsa) is a favorite, as it can be eaten with one hand while standing on a street corner. **"We're back in!"**

breast tape: Why do **Hollywood** actresses look different from the girl next door? They're not afraid to go the extra mile for beauty, including using what is basically Scotch tape to rearrange their cleavage. To uplift and separate, to . . . Well, you get the idea.

broadcast quality: An oxymoron. Before around 1990, there was a set of formal codified standards for video pictures bound for TV. You need so many lines of resolution, this sharpness, that level of signal, blah, blah, blah. Now pretty much anything goes, and they show home video, cop-car surveillance tapes; indeed, anything with a picture on it might find its way onto your TV. Better hide those naughty home videos.

brownie: Veteran motion-picture camera jockeys in **Hollywood** sometimes refer to the **camera body** as the brownie, a term adopted from the old Kodak still cameras of that name. Here's a great example of a term of obfuscation. When you ask for the brownie, almost no one in the world except for certain members of the **grip** or **camera department** will know what you're talking about. I told you there'd be some secret insider info in this book!

buck: (1) A buck is a reinforced wooden platform used to support **camera, actors,** lights, or scenery.

(2) A buck might also be slang for a car sawn in half (carefully) to facilitate filming **commercials**. Of course, the budget for the commercial spot increases a bit, as it's difficult to resell these chopped-up cars.

(3) In its most common usage, a buck is slang for a hundred of anything, as in, "Gimme a buck-and-a-half!" when asking for a 150 mm lens.

bump: A one-time bonus in pay offered to a movie worker in exchange for a special service rendered, such as a risky **stunt**, operating a **Steadicam**, or performing as a **special business extra**. *Ka-ching!*

business: No insightful financial advice here . . . sorry. *Business* actually refers to small bits of **action** performed during a **scene** that make the **actors'** performances more believable. In old **Hollywood** films, this generally consisted of smoking and drinking (see *The Thin Man* films). In today's finely crafted films, our **thespians** draw on other skills, and business consists of actresses brushing aside their hair and talking on cell phones . . . sometimes simultaneously!

C-47: Clothespins are used by the **electrics** to hold pieces of **gels** and **diffusion** onto hot lamps, but you'd look foolish asking a large **gaffer** for such a mundane household object. Better to refer to them by their cool secret West Coast movie name, the C-47.

cable: These garden-hose-thick rubberized copper wires connect the **genny** to the lights, **trailers**, trucks, hair dryers, anything on set requiring electricity. All the interconnected cables form a portable mini power grid, surrounding the **base camp** and **set**. At the end of each shoot day, the hardworking **electrics** put away all those heavy cables, and return the next day, at a new location, to start all over again. Ah, show business!

cable person: On a film shoot, this is the third person working on the sound crew. He or she is the right hand of the sound **mixer**, and helps the **boom operator** string along the various cables needed to link the actors' **mics** with the **sound cart**. If a second **boom pole** is needed (sometimes one microphone is not enough to cover the **action**), the cable person mans (or womans) it.

In a TV studio, the cable people wrestle with the thick, unwieldy cables emanating from the large studio video cameras.

callback: If they liked your first **audition** as an actor, you may be invited to a callback, which is yet another audition, every actor's dream! They like me! They really, really like me!

call sheet: The one-page template for the next day's work, handed out to all **crew** and cast members at **wrap**. The front side describes everything from **actors'** names, scenes to be filmed, props needed, the 2nd **AD's** personal phone number in case you get lost, as well as the most important piece of information: what time to come to work in the morning—the **call time**. On the back is a list of all **crew** and their specific job titles. Need to know what time to have those fifty wild horses ready for the roundup scene? It's on the call sheet.

call time: This is when the **crew** stops eating their **breakfast burritos** and starts working in the morning. Or in the evening. The movie **workday** might instead be a **split** or a **night call**.

cameo: When an established **star** takes a bit part in a film, it's called a cameo. Sometimes this is a character role, and at other times they simply play themselves. Director Alfred Hitchcock appeared briefly in nearly all his own films. Part of the fun in cameos is in recognizing the performers.

camera: For theatrical motion picture films, excellent 35 mm film cameras are made in the USA by **Panavision** in California, and in Europe by **Arri** and **Moviecam**. These are incredibly expensive (over two hundred thousand dollars when fully rigged) and are rented by the movie **company** for the duration of **principal photography** only. Digital **cinematography** is just now starting to challenge (at least in terms of picture quality) what had previously been the exclusive domain of the big three. Back to the drawing board.

camera 1: Often the live television studio maintains the **proscenium** and keeps the fourth wall of the **set** open. During a **multicamera** show, the TV director faces this stage, and beginning on his left the cameras at his disposal are very cleverly designated camera 1, camera 2, camera 3, and so on. He literally calls the shots into headsets worn by the camera crew. "Camera 3 . . . **pull back**, dammit!"

camera body: The **lens** and film **mags** attach to the body, a light-tight soundproof box filled with a bunch of gears and rollers, whose function it is to advance the filmstrip at a rate of ninety feet per minute. The first **AC** is responsible for the proper maintenance and adjustment of the film camera body. Similarly, a video or digital camera body is filled with a bunch of computer chips and wires, and in this case, a specialized video technician performs daily setup and maintenance.

camera department: Crew of highly trained personnel who tend to the movie camera equipment, usually between three and ten people depending on the budget. An average crew, in order of seniority is: **DP, camera operator, focus puller,** 2nd **AC,** and **loader.** A **still photographer** is ever present, to capture "behind the scenes" pictures and promotional material, and extra crew is added when using **multicamera** techniques.

camera head: Between the **camera body** and the **dolly** is the camera head. This is the geared mechanical contraption, manipulated by the very talented **camera operator,** that determines in which direction the **lens** is pointing. The smoothness of the resulting **shot** is largely dictated by the quality of the head and the abilities of the operator. A smaller, lighter **fluid head** can be substituted for the larger, more unwieldy **gear head** if space is at a premium or the operator reports to work with a hangover.

camera operator: Hey, that's me! The person pointing the **Panavision** camera at the movie stars. The **DP** lights the set, the **AC** is in charge of maintaining the equipment, and all the operator has to do is creatively execute the pictures from the director's imagination and keep the **actors** somewhere in the **frame**.

cans: Music-business and film-industry slang for headphones. Besides the **sound department,** other people may be found wearing cans on **set.** This includes anyone interested in hearing the actor's **dialogue,** such as the **director,** the **script supervisor,** and the **producers,** who spend most of their time in **video village**.

cans and bags: Opaque black bags and metal cans are supplied by the **lab** to the **camera department** for the safekeeping and transport of the valuable exposed film footage. A surefire funny practical joke on any movie set is for the **loader** to pretend to trip while carrying a full film can, and to let some old waste film go spooling across the **set.**

cappuccino: Did you know Guinness poured into a Starbucks coffee cup can be drunk with impunity right on a movie **set,** as the foam head looks exactly like cappuccino? Try this at the office on your job! You didn't hear it from me. And of course, if someone asks for a sip of your "coffee," you're in big trouble. See **fired**.

car rig: Refers to specialized **grip** equipment that affixes movie **cameras** to cars, such as suction cups, **speed rails,** and **hostess trays. Actors** for some reason find it difficult or impossible to drive with huge movie cameras mounted onto the hood of their cars. Better to use a tow rig. See **insert trailer.**

cardellini: When working in close quarters, lighting gear, **nets,** and **flags** can be mounted on a cardellini, a strong small clamp named for its inventor, Steve Cardellini of San Francisco. The **grip** package on any film contains dozens of **cardellinis**.

cast: The people in front of the camera—the **actors**, as opposed to the **crew**—who hide a safe distance out of view, behind the camera. We love our cast! On **location** for one film, I suggested a friendly softball game during a break in filming, cast versus crew. A burly grip piped up, "How about tackle football?"

casting: The art and science of deciding who gets to be in a movie and who will play which role. Final decisions are made by the **producers** and the **director**, aided by the **casting agent**.

casting agent: No doubt every actor attends far too many parties and **Hollywood** events in an attempt to meet one of these. The casting agent is a shortcut to stardom; they send thick books containing **actors' headshots** and bios to **directors** for consideration in hiring for specific roles. They also supply the **dayplayers** and **stand-ins** to movies in production.

casting couch: This refers to the alleged practice by some Hollywood producers and directors of furnishing an office with a couch, upon which would-be **actresses** perform special services in return for casting consideration. . . . You get the picture.

catering: Like the army, a movie **crew** travels on its stomach. Unlike an army, however, movie people refuse to eat MREs (army rations) or other prepackaged food. A gourmet caterer prepares hot meals for the twenty- to one-hundred-person film crew every six hours from a specially built and outfitted catering truck. Like prisoners on a desert island, much of the movie crew's spare time is taken up with discussions about food and catering.

catwalk: This is a wooden or metal walkway, which is suspended overhead on a movie **soundstage** and provides a working platform for adjusting scenery, lights, and similar equipment.

cattle call: Sometimes a movie **star** is cast after a single breakfast meeting with the **director** at a posh spot in Beverly Hills. Sometimes. The exact opposite of that is the cattle call. A notice announcing a casting call is placed in trade papers like *Variety* and *The Hollywood Reporter,* and dozens, hundreds, or even thousands of actors phone in sick to their respective jobs waiting tables and appear for a tryout. For the record, director Alfred Hitchcock never said that actors were cattle. He stated, "They should be *treated* like cattle." Well, at an open casting call, they are.

Cesar Award: French equivalent (sort of) of the **Academy Award**. Quick, name one film or actor who's won a Cesar! Now name an Oscar winner! See what I mean. The films that typically win Cesars exhibit that particularly French flair—adult relationships and sexual situations, middle-aged men who need a shave, and a lot of cigarette smoking. The other way to win a Cesar for your film project is to simply cast Gerard Depardieu . . . ze best!

CGI: Computer-generated image. Think . . . the dinosaurs in *Jurassic Park.* Actually, even a fairly straightforward movie these days will probably include several CG elements to enhance the footage. Rain, explosions, or even actors (Jar Jar Binks!) can be added later . . . for a price.

changed-elements clause: If an **above-the-line** person (**director, producer,** or **star**) drops out during the planning stages of a project, and then later Brad Pitt or someone really cool signs on, they can weasel their way back onto the film by invoking the changed-elements clause in their old contract. Wouldn't it be nice in the real world to get your old job back, anytime you want, after basically quitting? Only in **Hollywood.**

changing bag: When no **darkroom** is available for loading film **mags**, the film **loader** works with a large black rubberized canvas bag, which resembles a baggy wet suit top without the attached skin diver. The loader will stuff his or her arms deeply into this bag, along with film mags, **cans and bags**, large rolls of film, and scissors, emerging one to two minutes later with freshly loaded mags. *Voilà!* Movies can shoot up to one million feet of film. . . . That's a lot of changing rolls!

cheat: Any time an actor takes a position or leans in a way that is not entirely logical, it's termed a *cheat.* They do this at the request of the **director** or **DP** in order to make the resulting shot look more realistic. The **banana** is a good example of a common cheat. Also, furniture and **props** may be cheated, that is, rearranged slightly between shots to facilitate filming. Sometimes one can go too far, such as the time **commercial** director Elbert Budin got in hot water with the ad council watchdog groups for strategically placing a few large marbles into a bowl of Campbell's Soup to make it appear chunkier. Now that's cheating!

check the gate: At the end of every **setup** or filmed scene, the **AD** on a film set will shout, "Check the gate!" The whole **cast** and **crew** stands by while the 1st **AC** opens the camera **body** to check for errant bits of film **emulsion** called **"hairs."** Think of those squiggly white or black lines dancing on the screen during the projection of an old Fellini or Truffaut film at an art house cinema. On the set, if a **"Hair** in the gate!" is found (no one's fault, really), the camera will be quickly cleaned, the actors will regroup, and the previous **shot** will be refilmed immediately. And then . . . check the gate! Again.

chimera: The name of a mythical dragonlike beast, which is also the trade name for a portable nylon **diffusion** covering for movie lights. "Put a chimera on the **redhead**!" This can turn a **hardlight** with its highly directional light beam instantly into a **softlight**.

Chinese: This refers to a **camera** technique where the **dolly** is made smaller and turned sideways on the **track**. A **Dutch tilt**, a **ubangi**, a Chinese dolly—film workers have colorful ethnic nicknames for lots of things!

choker: An extremely tight **close-up**, usually showing only the **actor's** eyes, "the window to the soul." See any film by Sergio Leone. He does such tight shots of his star Clint Eastwood that the lines on his face look like the Grand Canyon.

chroma key: TV studio technique whereby a still picture, 2nd video source, or a background is electronically superimposed over the primary image. The **actors** are photographed in front of a blue, black, or bright green background and then electronically combined with the new elements. That's how local TV weather shows and old *Star Trek* episodes do it.

cinema verité: Fancy-ass French phrase meaning "**documentary.**" Every ten years or so, someone "reinvents" feature film style by incorporating **available light**, shaky **handheld** cameras, grainy footage . . . all established techniques of the nonfiction film. In the 1960s, it was the cinema verité (literally, "movie truth") of the French new wave (directors like Truffaut and Godard). Then came

Easy Rider, the Danish **Dogma** film movement, and *The Blair Witch Project*.

cinematographer: See **DP**. Often synonymous with cameraman (or camerawoman), this is the head of the motion-picture film **crew** during **principal photography**. They work quite closely with the **director**, helping them to capture their dreams on film, translating the director's flights of fancy into nuts-and-bolts **shots**. The close relationships that often develop may lead the director to use the same cinematographer on multiple projects.

cinematography: The art of photographing movies—it's as simple as that. From the time of **Edison** until now (one hundred years), this has meant capturing images on celluloid-based **emulsion**. Enter digital cameras . . .

cineplex: Going to the movies was once a social activity enjoyed by hundreds of viewers, sitting together in the dark, at an enormous single-screened movie "palace." These days one's cinema experience is limited to small, ugly carpeted boxes at the local mall. And the popcorn . . . so expensive!

Cinerama: The following definition includes Super Techniscope, Technirama, Panorama, Vista-Vision, and all other *ramas, scopes,* and *visions.* These were proprietary wide-screen photography and projection processes, an attempt during the 1950s and 1960s by **Hollywood studios** to compete with the rise of TV. Movie screens got wider, and TV is only now catching up, fifty years later. (New on NBC Television! High-definition wide-screen!) Each process had its own secret formula of lenses and cameras; the supply and demand of the marketplace sorted them out, and now for films we're left with just two standards, regular wide-screen and **anamorphic**. See also **aspect ratio**.

circled take: When the **director** sees the **actor** give a good performance, and there are no technical boo-boos by the **camera operator** and other technicians, the director asks the **script supervisor** to circle the take number in their report book. This is later passed on to the **lab** and the editors. The lab develops all the film that has been run through the camera each day, but it **prints** or sends to **film-to-tape** only the chosen circled takes. The rest of the film is safely stored away for a couple of years until it's time to cash in and release a **director's cut**.

clean entrance/exit: In order to give the **editor** options, **actors** often walk into camera view at the beginning of shots, and leave the **shot** (not necessarily the room) entirely before the **director** calls "cut" and the **camera operator** switches off the camera. Clean entrances and exits can help orient the viewer and create a believable world within the film.

clean track: This is a good-quality sound recording of the movie star's **dialogue**, unmarred by extra noises from behind the **camera**, such as laughs, coughs, farts, and the creaking sound a six-hundred-pound **dolly** makes when pushed across a hardwood **dancefloor**.

clear: When **crew** members scream this at each other on a working **set**, or the **catering** line, it means, "Get outta my way!" The other popular phrase is **"Watch your back!"** (Physically impossible.)

clear frame: During **setup**, this is what the **AD** will yell at slow-moving **crew** members who linger on the set. This is also what the

director yells at an **actor** during a **take**, when they want them to stop acting and leave the **shot**.

client: The big kahuna on **commercial** shoots, and easy to pick out—they're the only ones wearing suits. The client is the representative from the corporate world (Pepsi, Purina Cat Chow, or wherever) who signs the checks. They may not be up on all the latest fashions and cinematic slang (they need this book!), but we in the **crew** are all there to serve, and to make their stuff look yummy!

clone: Exact digital copy of a film or audio source. Ten tears ago, this was a dream. Now it's possible for the hundredth copy of a film to look and sound every bit as good as the original. No wonder the **Hollywood studios** are against file-sharing.

closed rehearsal: This is when the **crew** is invited to "get lost" for ten to fifteen minutes while the **actors** and **director** work out the **scene** to be filmed. **PAs** with **walkie-talkies** stand as sentries at the doorways to the **set**, encouraging the crew to "Keep quiet!" while they are "getting lost." After the closed rehearsal, the crew is invited to "get back to work" during the next step, the **blocking rehearsal**.

closed set: This is a bit different from a **closed rehearsal**. This is when all outsiders, and indeed most of the regular film **crew**, are excluded from the **set** whilst filming naked movie stars. Someone has to shoot it, of course, so the **camera operator** is always present, along with the 1st **AC**, the **boom operator**, and the **director**—that's the minimum. When adjustments to the **dolly**, lights, and so on are needed, the **cast** covers up with bathrobes, and crew members are called in. Some stars may be more skittish than others. When Julia Roberts (I knew she'd sneak her way into this book!) was asked to run down the hallway in her underwear on *Sleeping with the Enemy*, she reportedly requested that the entire working crew likewise strip down. One person (you know who you are) was found to be wearing large white boxer shorts printed with little red hearts.

close-up: A nice **shot** of an **actor's** face. Great care is spent in perfecting the **camera** angle and lighting when shooting close-ups. Actors know that faces tell the story of the film, and many save their best acting performances for these tight shots. After showing a brief **establishing shot**, whole TV programs consist almost entirely of close-ups, as the TV set in your living room is normally smaller than most movie screens (**cineplex** screens at the local mall excepted).

coffee: Forget about herbal tea or decaf—film crews drink tremendous amounts of coffee in order to maintain the necessary mental acuity and interest while working the long days and nights required. I would say the single most important element in maintaining crew morale (future **producers** take note) is having huge tanks of fresh coffee available all day long on the **craft service** table. Back when I managed a **soundstage**, my duties included making the breakfast. I learned there is simply no such thing as coffee that is too strong for a movie crew. That's what the milk is for, to cut it.

color: Color films have been around for a long time; in the 1910s and 1920s filmmakers would sometimes laboriously hand-tint individually each frame of film. Then in the 1940s came the **Technicolor** process, making color possible for any **producer** willing to pay a little extra. In the late 1950s use of color became nearly universal. Now, with digital effects and **editing** systems, we have nearly complete control over every shade of color for our completed film projects. The Lord of the Rings films were shot in New Zealand (a very colorful and green country, by the way), yet the finished film has an overall gray cast to it, not quite **day-for-night**, but subtly dark and foreboding. A couple of mouse clicks can flavor the whole film.

color correction: In this process, an entire **feature** or TV **show** is examined by a skilled technician in a controlled environment, such as a **postproduction house,** and working under the direction of the **DP,** shot-by-shot minute corrections are made in **exposure, framing,** and color balance. All feature films go through this process after editing, during a **film-to-tape** transfer; it takes from one to four days to plow through an entire film during final color correction.

color temperature: One of the few times where strong math skills are called for in movies. Without getting too technical, the color temperature of daylight is 5,600 degrees Kelvin, artificial movie lamps can be 5,600 or 3,200 degrees K, and the **gaffer** and **DP** plan accordingly. (Did I lose anybody?) Simply put, some light out there is **blue,** and some is orange, and, unlike the human eye, film and video cameras are quite sensitive to the differences. Color temperatures are a way to assign relative numbers to these color values. Phew!

color timer: The employee of the film **lab** whose job it is to make sure the **actors** look their best and all the colors in the film match. This is the celluloid film equivalent of video **color correction.** The timer might work all day or stay up all night printing the **dailies** for the shooting **crew.**

colorizing: Ted Turner and others of little or no taste sometimes add color digitally to classic **black-and-white** films. This was popular a few years back, though since we are now continually bombarded with digitally manipulated images of all types, much of the hoopla has faded. I mean, if we have computerized Jurassic Park dinosaurs chowing down on real **actors**, adding a little color to Humphrey Bogart's cheeks seems like no big deal.

commercial: Thirty-second mini-movies, which predominate network and cable television and are now also shown in movie theaters before feature films. The same highly trained **freelance** movie crews may also work on commercials. The work process is exactly the same, but whereas Francis Coppola may take two to three hours to explore the various **themes** on *Apocalypse Now Redux,* he's got thirty seconds to develop a story line, create memorable characters, and sell some freakin' dog food on an Alpo spot.

company move: This phrase is shouted out by the **PAs** when a **scene** has been completed. Time to load the trucks. A film may require several moves in a day, or might stay put at one **location** for a week. Better check the **advance schedule**.

the company: Washington, D.C., slang for the CIA, in films this is the all-encompassing name for everyone being employed making the film. If the CIA hired a surveillance film crew, would they be the company company?

Comtek: These are little wireless headphones, worn by the **director, script supervisor,** and the **producers** on the **set**, that allow them to listen to the live sound of the actors' voices. Comteks are necessary for these citizens of **video village,** as simply hearing the actors' voices on **location** becomes difficult. The camera and **props** crews will conspire to place the **director's chairs** twenty to thirty feet away from the camera and actors, to keep producers, with all their helpful "suggestions," safely at a distance.

concept artist: When a film has a cool unique look (like in *Star Wars*, *The Fifth Element*, *Alien*), it's likely the **producers** sprang for the services of a talented concept artist.

construction coordinator: Oversees all set building. Need the *Temple of Doom* set finished over the weekend? Better make pals with the construction coordinator. And bring a checkbook.

construction grips: They often know about an upcoming project before anyone else, sometimes even the **director**. They're hired by the **producer** well in advance of the film, and are hard at work building **sets** weeks ahead of the **principal photography**.

contingency: On a **commercial,** this is the extra money the savvy **producer** builds into the budget in case "shit happens," like crew overtime or rainy weather. On a feature film, this is (rare) left-over money in the budget sometimes used by the **director** for **reshoots**.

continuity: The difficult art of crafting a believable whole story from the many elements and shots while the film's being photographed. The **script supervisor** leads this quest. **Eyelines, prop** placements, actor movements, hemlines, hairstyles, and cigarette lengths—all of these and more have to match as closely as possible from shot to shot.

cookie: Not something to eat and not a sneaky little invasive computer program, *cookie* refers to a cukaloris, a special **flag** that creates nice shadow patterns when placed in front of a light. A natural branch from a tree provided by the **greensman** for this purpose is termed a *branchaloris*.

costume: For you and me at home, it's called clothing. In movies, the outfit makes the character, so talented people spend a lot of time choosing the right wardrobe for the **thespians**. Note the difference between Austin Powers and Dr. Evil. Same actor, new costume.

costume designer: Executing the **director's** wishes and keeping in mind the movie star's ego, they oversee the wardrobe department, buying or making from scratch all the outfits to be worn **on-screen**. Sometimes after a shoot is over, you can buy slightly used movie clothes cheaply from **the company**! A friend of mine has Robert Duvall's *Lonesome Dove* hat. I myself have some of Harvey Keitel's bowling shirts. Now I just need some shoes. . . .

cover set: If the day's intended work outside is rained out, it may be time to load up the trucks and move to the cover set, shooting an entirely different **scene** on a prepared **soundstage**. The decision whether or not to go "to cover" is made by the **producer**. After all, it's their money. Frantic cell phone calls will be made to ensure that **props, sets,** and **actors** are ready to film the new scene.

coverage: These are additional shots filmed after the **master shot** is **in the can**, which "cover" the **director's** butt later on during editing, when it becomes necessary to assemble a coherent story from many different camera angles. These might be **cutaways, cowboys, full shots,** or **close-ups.**

cowboy: A type of character actor last employed by the big movie **studios** in 1958. Actually, there are some good Westerns made these days, and they're required to feature either Clint Eastwood or Gene Hackman, or both. In **camera** lingo, a cowboy is a shot that frames both an **actor** and his gun (should he be wearing one). A cowboy shot is wider than a **close-up**, but not quite a **full shot**.

crab: This is when the **dolly grip** pushes the film camera **dolly** sideways, all four wheels pointing in the same direction. The corresponding video term for this is *truck,* and the **camera operator** pushes the camera around himself, unaided by a grip. A TV director might say, "Camera 3, truck to the right, dammit!"

craft service: One of the perks of working on movies is the readily available unhealthy food and drink of the craft-service table. One or two craft-service people have the sole responsibility of tending to the daily grazing needs of the rest of the **crew**, providing everything from **coffee** and doughnuts to sunscreen and vitamins. You know, a person could probably live off craft service. See **radio-man**.

crane: The camera is sometimes placed on a long **boom** arm controlled by the **grips** in order to facilitate high-angle shots. The camera, two seats, the **camera operator**, the **focus puller**, **batteries**, **cables**, and two cups of coffee are all mounted at one end, and lead counterweights are placed in a steel basket at the other end. It's basically a gigantic thirty-foot seesaw, and is more than a little unwieldy. In the last few years, unmanned **remote heads** have become more popular.

Crank-O-Vator: A really big lighting stand, adjusted by turning a really big crank handle. This gets the lighting unit up high; just make sure you **sandbag** it. On a windy day in Boston on the film *Once Around,* I got mashed by a falling light and was sent off to the hospital on a backboard. Not good.

credits: Even veteran **crew** members feel a little zing of pride when they see their names up there on the big screen. That's the problem with working on **commercials**: There's no time to show credits. If your name comes before the film and appears onscreen by itself (a **main title credit**), you're probably a movie **star, art director, editor, costume supervisor, writer,** music composer, **DP, producer,** or the film's **director.** Chances are you sat in a **director's chair** with your name on it during shooting. Everyone else, from **key grip** to animal **wrangler,** is listed in the end credits.

crew: Not the rich **producers,** and not the pampered **actors,** these are the dozens of people who work hard every day to handcraft the film. Films divide roughly into management, cast, and crew, with the crew doing most of the heavy lifting. Have you read the **credits?** It takes between 50 and 150 people all pulling together so James Cameron can proclaim himself "king of the world" and win an **Oscar.**

crew jacket: At the conclusion of **principal photography,** the producer customarily buys each **crew** member a **wrap gift,** which generally takes the form of a nice outdoor jacket. When worn on the **"next big one,"** these crew jackets can serve as conversational icebreakers: "You worked on *Scooby-Doo*?" I still have my Waldorf-Astoria bathrobe given to me on *Scent of a Woman*. Wait a minute . . . maybe I stole that one.

crew van: The cameras and lights travel between locations in trucks, but the shooting **crew** packs into vans. Whether **scouting** future locations or just grabbing a lift to **catering,** riding in the crew van provides an opportunity to discuss important filmmaker stuff, or to just exchange gossip. The confined space, the captive audience, and the long drives can breed some great "war stories." Director-writer David Mamet reportedly based his film *State and Main* entirely on stories overheard while riding around in crew vans.

cross the line: One of the main rules of filmmaking, handed down by Moses to C. B. DeMille during *The Ten Commandments*. Thou shalt *not* cross the line. In a nutshell, within a scene, actor A looks to the left, and in another shot actor B looks back at them to the right. A **line of force** is drawn between the two people, and all the camera placements need to take place on only *one* side of this line. Cross the line by putting the camera in the wrong place, and all hell breaks loose; it's like driving your car down the highway on the wrong side. See also **screen direction**.

C-stand: Short for *century stand* (West Coast slang), another name for **grip stand** (East Coast slang), which is a gangly large metal apparatus on an adjustable tripod base, designed to hold **flags** and **nets**. These are artfully placed around the **set** by the **grips,** as directed by the **DP**, to modify light beams (create shadows).

CTO: Color temperature orange. All film lighting gear is divided into daylight (blue) and **tungsten** (orange). See **eighty-five** for a fuller explanation. CTO often denotes an orange **gel,** placed in front of a light that renders the resulting light beam "warmer," like late-afternoon sunshine.

cube tap: To get one at the hardware store, you'd have to ask for a three-to-two electrical plug adapter.

cue: On the movie set, a cue is the signal for something to happen, such as the **director** or **AD** goosing the **actors** or **background** to begin acting.

On a video shoot, sometimes the director or **technical director** will say "Cue!" instead of the more popular phrase **"Action!"** to start things happening.

In the **sound department,** *cue* is a verb meaning "to swing the **mic** around overhead," in order to pick up the **dialogue** of more than one actor.

cue card: When an actor can't remember his or her **lines,** the lines are written down on a large white **show card** and held just out of view of the camera lens. Cue cards are rarely used on movies (we can **cut** the camera, and an **actor** has several takes to get the words right), but are occasionally used on TV, especially during live events such as NBC's *Saturday Night Live.* Also see **teleprompter.**

cut: Traditionally only the **director** gets to yell "Cut!" to stop the filming. They get a little touchy if a person stops the camera a tiny touch too soon on "their" film. While filming *The Associate,* Whoopi Goldberg's character was named Cutty. Guess what yours truly did when I heard the director shout "Cutty!" Oops! One exception to the director-God-cut rule is during a **stunt** when the **stunt coordinator** is in charge.

cut to the chase: Here's an example of a phrase that originated on movies and now is used only in general conversation. Today it means "get to the point," but at one time, it referred to the standard movie plot, where tension builds during an exciting finishing sequence.

cutaway: A cutaway is a brief **shot** that is not really linked to the rest of the action, such as an **insert** of a gun, or a car tire peeling out. On an action picture, these can really help build the overall flavor of a scene, and such neutral shots help bridge gaps in the **action.** Sec-

ond unit crews are often called in to film cutaway shots, usually without the presence of the highly paid stars themselves.

cutter: (1) Older film-industry people sometimes refer to **editors** as cutters, though these days, the film isn't physically "cut" so much as digitally rearranged.

(2) On **set**, cutter refers to a black **flag** artistically placed by **grips** to cast a shadow, or *cut* the light.

cutting room floor: In the good old days of film's first one hundred years, until **Avid** and **Final Cut Pro** editing systems took over completely, unused celluloid scenes were physically trimmed by the movie's **editor** and ended up—guess where? A future actor's lament: "My best scenes ended up on the eighty-gigabyte number two hard drive!"

cyc: Pronounced *psych*. Short for *cyclorama,* the cyc is where the rear wall on a **soundstage** blends in a graceful curve with the studio floor, instead of being set at a right angle. Curved cycs are used on countless **product shots** and **commercial** photo shoots. If a smaller smooth, curved background is needed, a piece of **seamless** paper will do the trick.

dailies: Film shot the previous day is viewed in a **screening room** by the **director** and assorted **crew**, though not by the **actors**. Most directors don't want them to become self-conscious or alter their performances . . . plus they need their beauty sleep. Dailies are an essential part of the filming process; they can help shortcut any mistakes. Though viewing dailies only on videotape seems cost-effective, take a lesson from George Lucas. While filming *Star Wars: Episode I* he was "saving money" by watching his dailies on a small video screen, only to discover weeks later that he had to **reshoot** many of the **close-ups** due to technical problems. Ouch!

dancefloor: This refers to the smooth temporary floor surface, quickly built by **grips**, to ensure a smooth ride for the **dolly** (put down in five to fifteen minutes—using a chain saw helps move things along). Dancefloors are generally made of high-quality plywood, which can afterward be resold or taken home by **crew** members (and made into kitchen cabinets!).

darkroom: On a movie filming on a **soundstage**, the **loader** works in a telephone booth–size pitch-black room, switching **raw stock** for exposed film in the **mags**. The potential for disaster is great, as all the film (representing the day's work of more than one hundred people) literally passes through the loader's hands in the darkroom. Please knock before entering!

dawn: If the script calls for a dawn shot, the actual filming often takes place at sunset instead. Here's why: Dust and pollution kicked up by the earth's inhabitants during the day usually make for a much prettier and more prolonged sunset than sunrise. It's also easier to assemble the photo-ready **cast** and **crew** at 6 p.m., rather than 6 a.m.

day of days: This is a slightly more detailed **shooting schedule** than a **one-liner**. The day-of-days schedule optimistically states the **page count** to be completed, as well as serving as a kind of countdown to the ultimate **wrap**. Each day of photography is given a number ("The **grips** need the **crane** on Day 8, and we need to find a new caterer for Days 6 to 21!"), and this is always compared to the number of days allotted in the budget. When you **run over**, you might find yourself filming day ninety-nine out of thirty-seven.

day/ext: Daytime exterior. This is shorthand for a **scene** meant to look like daytime, filmed outdoors. Of course, the scene conceivably might be filmed on the corner of a **soundstage** in the middle of the night with artificial lights and a few trees strategically placed by the **greensman**, but it will still be called day/ext.

day/int: Daytime interior. **Scenes** filmed during daytime indoors, whether in someone's house or on a **soundstage**, are noted as day/int. Shining big movie lights in through the windows can extend the workday for the crew far into the evening hours. Better cancel those dinner plans. . . .

day-for-night: The title of a great movie about filmmaking by François Truffaut. (Head for Blockbuster!) Interestingly what we in **Hollywood** call day-for-night is termed "American night" by French movie crews. In many old American Westerns, the crew filmed during midday and tried, with varying degrees of success, to make it look like moonlight. This is filming day-for-night. Lighting up large out-door areas at nighttime just wasn't practical in those days. Now we have some big-ass movie lights and **fast film**. Today day-for-night is only occasionally attempted. Secret techniques, which help enhance the effect, include underexposing the film, using blue or gray **filters**, and keeping the camera angle high to avoid showing the bright sky.

dayplayer: Refers to any **cast** or **crew** person hired on a day-to-day basis. The great big dysfunctional family that is a Hollywood film in progress is divided into groups of people hired yearly (L.A. studio employees), people hired for **the run of the show** (cast and crew), and dayplayers.

deal memo: This is the one-page quasi-legal agreement between the producer and an individual **crew** member, which spells out the **rate** of pay and conditions of employment. In these politically correct times, you are often asked to sign statements renouncing discrimination of all kinds, and sexual harassment as well. Not a problem.

deep focus: In the 1940s on his great film *Citizen Kane,* director Orson Welles decided to challenge the rules of movie physics and have everything in the camera's view appear sharply in **focus**. He did this by utilizing only **wide-angle** lenses and by pouring a ton of light onto the **set**. This allowed for a small lens **aperture**. The film, pho-tographed by Gregg Toland, ASC, was a landmark and is still admired by both film students and professional filmmakers. Film **directors** at-tempting deep focus today should be prepared to spend a fortune on extra lights, extra crew, extra time . . . just as Welles did back then. See also **depth of field** (some math required).

demo reel: Freelance camerapeople, **art directors**, **actors**, even **directors** get work assignments by showing **producers** a half-inch

VHS, DVD, or three-quarter-inch videotape of their previous work. If you're Spielberg or the Coen Brothers, you can suggest a trip to any **cineplex**, but for others, the demo reel is the way to get noticed.

department: Film workers fit into parallel hierarchies, just like workers in any other business. For example: **props** department, sound department, or editing department. It's all a matter of knowing who belongs where. The **camera operator** belongs to the camera department, but the fellow moving the camera to make a **shot**, the **dolly grip**, belongs to the grip department and answers to his boss, the **key grip**.

depth of field: This is important stuff. The part of a **shot** in sharp **focus** is said to fall within the accepted depth of field. Only four factors affect the depth of field and the apparent sharpness of any photographic image: (1) **format** (16 mm film, 35 mm film, video, large-format still camera, whatever), (2) **focal length** of the lens—wide-angle or telephoto, (3) subject-to-camera distance—how far away is the actor?, (4) **iris** setting—**f-stop**—of the lens. These are the four elements that are manipulated to control focus and sharpness in the final picture. Orson Welles worked with numbers two and four to achieve his famous **deep focus** effect. Here's another example: If the **close-up** shot of Tom Cruise is out of focus, or "soft," someone probably made a mistake concerning number three. See **focus puller, fired**.

DGA: The Directors Guild of America represents **directors, ADs, PAs,** and some other production positions. Though not really a hiring hall, the DGA functions as a **union**, negotiating better conditions, a health plan, and mo' money for its members.

DGA trainee: To join the **DGA**, you can either document a certain number of official union workdays as a **PA** over several years, or you might choose to sign up for the DGA training program. An established **AD** will take you under his wing, show you the ropes, and train you to someday take over his job.

dialogue: Spoken lines are the difference between the old silent movies and "talkies." Dialogue is scripted by the **screenwriter** weeks or months before shooting begins, and even great actors like Meryl Streep and Robert De Niro stick pretty much to the **script**. Sometimes the director might allow some **improv**, but what sounds smart and funny **on the day** might fall flat in the **screening room**. I worked on a film for Miramax, where the actors (Roseanne, Michael J. Fox, Lou Reed, Mira Sorvino, Harvey Keitel, Giancarlo Esposito) were encouraged to make up their own lines. The film was titled *Blue in the Face*. Did you see it? No. See what I mean?

diffusion: Large **frames** of paper or fabric, with secret names like 216, 250, silk, gryff, and parachute, are placed in the path of harsh light beams to soften the overall effect. Anything used for this purpose is termed diffusion. **Filters**, petroleum jelly (old-timey Hollywood trick), black stockings, and other schmutz placed on the **lens** in an attempt to make an older actress look like her younger self, are likewise termed diffusion. Recently Mary Tyler Moore produced and starred in a new *Mary and Rhoda* TV movie, and she wanted to set the clock back twenty-five years to when she first played the role of Mary Richards. Let's just say I had so much diffusion on the lens, I could barely see through the camera.

dig it out: AD shorthand for "Please, sir, would you and those nice **grip** gentlemen mind moving all those heavy items? They might unintentionally appear in the next **shot**."

digital artist: A **postproduction** digital artist using computers creates that which is impossible, or expensive, to produce live on the **set**. This might entail placing the **actors** in a new background, such as the Himalayas (it's difficult talking people into spending two months on location in Kathmandu), or even creating actors totally from scratch (Jar Jar Binks!).

dimmer: Electricians often plug the **movie lights** into large portable dimmers (rheostats, or variacs) to control the light level, just as you might use to create a romantic lighting effect with the ceiling light at home. Your eye probably doesn't see it, but this also makes the resulting light appear a bit more orange.

dingle: A dingle is an artistic little splash of light, such as a metallic reflection, created by talented **DPs** and **gaffers** at great effort and expense. A big dingle gone out of control might become a highlight, and then when all control is lost, a **flare**.

diopter: A glass **filter** temporarily screwed onto the end of a **lens** to enable **macro** (close focus) shots. Also called a proxar. Diopter is also the adjustment on the end of the camera eyepiece that accommodates different people's corrected vision needs. Your eyeglass prescription is a diopter rating, such as +1 or +2.25. By dialing a knob on the eyepiece, the **camera operator** or **director** can see a sharp image without wearing glasses.

direct address: Actors never look directly at the camera. This is one of the cardinal rules of **narrative** filmmaking. TV news anchors and spokesmodels, however, look right into the lens and engage the audience in direct address. Sometimes one can use this for a heightened effect on TV shows and movies (watch Bernie Mac, for example, or any film with John Cusack), but it's used sparingly because it draws attention to technique, not text, and can shock the audience out of a carefully crafted fictional film world.

director: This is the best job in the world. You know what a director is, the creative boss, the person making the movie. On every working movie **set,** the tone of the workplace filters down from the daily attitude and mood of the director. A confident chief leads to a calm, professional set (Sidney Lumet, Jonathan Demme), a funny person directing a comedy makes all our jobs enjoyable (Betty Thomas, Dennis Dugan), and a paranoid control freak like [*names omitted—legal dept.*].

director's chair: You know you've arrived at the top of the **Hollywood** heap when you get a portable chair on the **set** with your name on it. In addition to his or her other duties, the **prop master** is charged with setting up folding canvas chairs for the most important people on the set, including the **director, producers, executive producers, DP, continuity supervisor,** and the lead **actors.** Tip: Never sit in someone else's director's chair. That's not *your* name on it. Director John Badham caught me sitting in his chair, reading a newspaper on *The Hard Way,* and banished me to **second unit** for a week!

director's cut: It's much easier and more profitable to simply rerelease your old film than to shoot a new original work. You can put all the long boring scenes back into the film, thanks to easy digital editing systems, and call it the director's cut. This makes a pile more money for the **producers** and **directors**. The crew who worked long hours crafting the film? Zip. Zero. Nada. Many years ago I worked on *Dirty Dancing,* and when they rereleased it to theaters for the ten-year anniversary, all the producer had to do was make some new **prints**. No extra money for me. And the director had been dead for three years.

director's finder: This is the small optical tube worn around the neck that aids **directors** and **DPs** in envisioning **shots**. No need to drag the heavy **dolly** and camera around, guessing at camera placements. Of course, if you don't have a director's finder, you can always do the Hollywood cliché by squinting through your fingers on an outstretched hand.

director's notes: These are verbal "suggestions" given to actors by the director after a less-than-perfect **take.**

dirty close-up: Not what you think at all, you naughty reader! This is a variation of the **over-the-shoulder** shot that is more of a **close-up** and less of a **medium shot**. A dirty close-up is a tight shot of actor A, into which actor B (the one with his back to the camera) intrudes, sometimes obscuring a bit of the main subject altogether. Just don't lean into actor A's close-up too far. That's termed **blocking,** and he or she may retaliate.

dissolve: A transitional device used when editing. One **shot** fades out, and as a new one fades in, the two are briefly superimposed over each other. Typically used to indicate a passage of time and to smooth transitions between two dissimilar shots. Francis Coppola makes long dissolves part of the storytelling style during the early scenes of his great film *Apocalypse Now,* in order to create a descriptive portrait of Martin Sheen's character, Captain Willard.

distribution: The business of releasing a film to be shown in movie theaters. Shooting a film can be costly, but distributing thousands of finished copies of the film around the country for exhibition is *really* expensive. Sometimes films are completed and then struggle to find a **studio** willing to fund this **theatrical release**. See **straight to video**.

documentary: Whatever you do, don't use the D-word when **pitching** your movie idea to a prospective **producer**. Say "reality-based narrative drama" instead. Film documentaries are notoriously difficult and expensive to produce, relative to any perceived potential profits. The line between documentary and narrative fiction gets more blurred every year. Some documentaries are well made, intricately crafted, and are bloody good entertainment (see any film by Errol Morris). Reality-based TV **shows**, such as planting cameras all around a girls' college dorm, are another way to go.

Dogma: This is a name taken by a group of Danish and European film directors willing to sign a "manifesto" dating to 1995, stating they would shoot their films in the future with no "Hollywood" tricks. Instead, all films had to be photographed with only natural lighting, handheld cameras—no dollies, no sets, no "superficial" action such as gunplay and stunts . . . basically rejecting everything I believe in!

Dolby: Why does the name Dolby appear in huge letters on the screen before nearly every movie? Let's see . . . Ray Dolby was born in Portland in 1933, helped develop the videotape recorder for Ampex when he was twenty years old, received a Ph.D. in Physics from Cambridge in 1961, served as consultant to the fledgling British Atomic Energy program, became United Nations Advisor to India, and then founded Dolby Laboratories in London in 1966, where he still runs things. Dolby greatly improved cinema by developing sophisticated noise-reduction systems for movie **soundtracks**. Just thought you might want to know.

dolly: Not at all like the furniture dolly you might use to move the refrigerator. The German word describes it perfectly: *Kamerawagen*. It's the sofa-size heavy rolling contraption that supports the movie camera and **camera operator**, and is pushed by the **dolly grip**. Good dollies are made by Chapman or Fisher in Hollywood. The dolly usually rolls around on carefully placed **track** or a plywood **dancefloor**. Accessories for the dolly include such items as **risers**, sideboards, and slightly larger platforms termed "elephant ears." **Grips** tend to be quite creative with nicknames.

dolly grip: Specifically, the person in charge of guiding the **dolly**, which holds the camera, the **camera operator**, and often the **focus puller** while filming. The dolly grip prepares the track or **dancefloor** and then works the dolly or **crane**. The job calls for a mix of the artistic and mechanical, as the dolly grip has to be in tune with the **actors** while filming, hit **marks** with precision, and anticipate any surprises.

doorway dolly: A small lightweight **western dolly** that has a flat platform covered in plywood and felt, and is outfitted with small pneumatic tires. It's named for its ability to fit between narrow doorjambs, but they're a little unstable for filming, so many **grip** crews use them to transport **sandbags** instead.

dots and fingers: Very small **flags**, most often used when very carefully lighting a small **set**, such as on a **commercial**.

double: A double-thick wire **scrim** placed in front of a spotlight to reduce its intensity by approximately half. Color code is red. If you have a round scrim in your hand that's green, it's a **single**.

double take: The acting technique whereby the **thespian** doesn't immediately respond to another actor's look or **line**, but rather waits a **beat** and then responds . . . usually for comic effect. Cary Grant is the master of the stylish double take.

double time: In jazz music, this is when the band swings into full gear and plays at twice the tempo. On a movie crew, *double time* means you've worked a very long day already, and are now earning twice the hourly wage . . . *ka-ching!*

doughnut: Round fattening pastries on the **craft-service** table beloved by all crew. *Doughnut* is also camera slang for a circular piece of rubber foam that fits between the **lens** and the **sunshade** on the camera, and looks exactly like its sugary baked counterpart. Just don't confuse the two.

download: This is how movies will be distributed in the future. The neighborhood theater will probably survive (everyone likes to get out of the house, sometimes), but the files containing the movie picture and sound information will be beamed directly from large computer servers at the **studios** via high-speed cable or satellite to local venues, whether the **cineplex** or your house. Once big reels of film are unnecessary, and all movies (not just bootleg DVDs) are digitized, piracy of the files will become an issue. Watch for the movie studios to come out big in the fight against personal computer file-sharing. From the studios' point of view, their very existence is at stake.

downstage: Director's note given to an **actor** by the **director** meaning to come closer to the camera. "Bring it downstage, Sandler!" This term comes from the old days of theater, when stages sloped downward toward the audience, enabling everyone to have a clear view. Now we have stadium-style seating at the **cineplex** for the same reason.

DP: Director of Photography. Works under the **director** and is the head of the **crew,** in charge of photographing the film. They are the ultimate authorities on lighting, **lens** choice, **filters,** film **exposure,** and they have a lot of input into choosing **locations,** set design, and almost every aspect of the film. Anybody can simply take pictures, but movies such as *The Godfather, Apocalypse Now,* and *Lawrence of Arabia* are *created* from thin air by the **DP** (or cinematographer). Good DPs command a lot of respect and a healthy salary. On the other hand, the DP is one of the people most likely to get fired from a movie when "creative differences" with the director or **producer** arise.

draftsman: Person who translates the ideas or sketches of the **production designer** into line drawings from which the **construction grips** can assemble, build, conjure the movie's **sets.**

drive-by shot: Nothing to do with firearms or gangs, a drive-by is a **shot** where the **hero** car simply drives by the camera position as the **camera operator** gets whiplash trying to keep it in **frame.**

dub: A term coming from our friends in the **sound department,** a dub is short for overdub, the process by which a new line of **dialogue,** sound effect, or musical bit is added after the fact.

Release prints of films are often dubbed into other languages; the voices of native speakers are added after the film has been completed. The great Italian director Federico Fellini supposedly let his actors **improv** in whatever language they wanted. He knew he would piece together the **scene** in **editing** and add dubbed dialogue later. Audiences over here are less forgiving of dubbed movies, and great pains are taken to record a **clean track** on **Hollywood** movies. On the silver screen, we like to see Americans speaking American.

dulling spray: Dozens of cans of dulling spray, a matte finish spray available at any art supply store, are used on the average movie. Under the direction of the **DP**, or the **camera operator**, a **prop** person applies a fine mist to shiny objects on the **set** that otherwise would draw attention away from the **actors**. Parked cars are frequent targets for dulling. Just be sure you clean up the sticky residue—or leave the area before the surprised or disgruntled car owner appears.

dupe: Duplicate. The process (verb) or end result (noun) of making additional copies of video- and audiotapes. In analog media, such as magnetic audiotape or VHS video, copies are never as good as the original source material. In the new digital age, exact copies are possible with no loss of quality, and these are called **clones**.

Dutch: As if innovations such as wooden shoes and windmills weren't enough, the tilting of a movie camera to one side is termed a Dutch angle. Normally, the tripod or **dolly** is carefully leveled. A Dutch tilt cants the camera to the side, and this is used for a dramatic effect. (Look closely at any car **commercial**.) I used this technique quite a bit on Universal Studios' *Virus* to simulate the ship's rolling during a hurricane.

Duvatyne: Another essential building block of film, multipurpose rolls of black fabric. Stretched on frames, Duvatyne makes **flags**. Hung from overhead, it becomes a **teaser**. Taped to a shiny car, it kills the **flare**. When draped over **crew** members in an improvised Duvatyne poncho, it serves as an invisibility cloak for filming around glass and mirrors.

E

earbud: An earbud is a small receiver worn in the ear to enable actors to hear the beat of the music during a dance scene. Or in the case of late great actor Marlon Brando on a recent film, to hear the **script supervisor** feed him **dialogue** he couldn't be bothered to memorize, like a high-tech Cyrano de Bergerac.

ECU: Extreme close-up, **choker**, tight shot. The window to the soul may be the eyes; just keep in mind that the closer you are to the object being photographed, the harder it is to keep things in **focus**. (See Dave's rule #3 under **depth of field**.)

edge of frame: Now here's another term of essential film grammar. Most viewers are conditioned to look at the action taking place in the center of a filmed picture. That's why people jump when presented with a shark or whatever appearing suddenly from **offscreen**. Skilled filmmakers will often create tension and interesting compositions by placing objects and actors not just smack in the middle, but near the edge of **frame**.

edison: New Jersey's own Thomas Edison figures prominently in the birth of the movies. Working alone, he invented from scratch everything we need for movies: electric lights, microphones, phonograph sound recording, and the motion-picture camera. Nice résumé! It took George Eastman to figure out how to get *film* into the camera, however. On the **set**, an **edison** is the term used for a standard three-pronged household electrical plug.

editing: To remove all the film or video that is unnecessary to telling the film's story, leaving only the choice bits. Well, that's what you do at first when editing a **rough cut**. These days, the process of editing is more nearly synonymous with **postproduction** and includes editing the film, waiting for the visual effects to be ready, mixing the sound, rerecording bits of dialogue, waiting for the visual effects to be ready, adding the music, putting in the now-ready visual effects, test screening, and the like.

editor: The editor and assistants occasionally visit the film being shot on the **set**, but they normally have their own high-tech suite loaded with computer equipment. Editors report directly to the producer and director. Their first task is preparing the **dailies**. Sometimes they hurriedly prepare a **trailer** that **previews** the film in question for movie audiences and the **studio**. When **principal photography** is complete, the editor assembles a **rough cut** version, which the **director** later either changes completely or adopts wholesale (and for which he then takes credit). This is called collaboration.

effects: See the 1986 movie *FX,* starring Bryan Brown, for a great depiction of a live special-effects crew at work on set. They use movie tricks to fool the cops and steal a lot of money. Woo-hoo!

effects house: This refers to **postproduction** specialty facilities, such as **ILM** (Industrial Light & Magic), which might be hired to provide flying spacecraft shots or dinosaurs for a film. Can't figure out how to do a difficult **shot** on **set**? Farm it out to an effects house.

EFX: Short for **effects**; see above.

eggcrate: Large crisscross metal frames that attach to the front of a movie lamp and look like, well, a giant black metal eggcrate. These help direct and control the powerful light beam generated by 10,000-kilowatt movie lights.

eighty-five/85: Unlike video cameras and the superbly adaptable human eye, film is extremely sensitive to color differences. When shooting in daylight, often an 85 **filter** is used in front of the camera **lens**. It looks strongly orange to the naked eye, but renders the scene on film quite naturally. Sometimes large sheets or rolls of 85 **gel** (aka **CTO**) are affixed to windows by the **grips** for the same reason. Just remember 85 = **CTO** = orange.

electric: There are normally between two and ten of these electricians working on the film, the head person being the **gaffer**. An electric might do everything from delicately adjusting a lamp for the **DP** on a quiet **set**, wrestling with the heavy electrical **cable** used for power, or manning a light placed on a **snorkel lift** and dangling overhead the **actors** for six hours straight. Ah, the glamour of show business!

Elemack: A brand of four-wheeled Italian **dolly**, the principal attraction of which is a camera **riser** set on a tall base. Of course, this makes low shots difficult, and only crafty European **camera operators** and **grip** crews have figured out how *not* to spin around uncontrollably during long dolly moves. See also **Panther**.

emulsion: Film, whether it's movie film or the Kodak brand you put in your camera at home, consists of a clear base layer with some light-sensitive silver crystals sandwiched to it. That's the emulsion. Light streams in through the camera's **lens**, and voilà! Another timeless image is captured.

endslate: Also called *tailslate, endmark,* or *tailboard.* Sometimes the camera crew will clap the marking **slate** at the conclusion  of a **shot,** not at the beginning. It's common practice to endslate when animal actors or children are involved. One can also offer to endslate if the dramatic actor's concentration might be broken by the loud banging of two pieces of wood near the face.

EQ: This term, courtesy of the **sound department,** is short for *equalization:* the adjustment of bass and treble frequencies on the **soundtrack** to optimize sound quality. Can't hear Whoopi's jokes? Need Schwarzenegger's voice to sound more threatening? Slap some EQ on it!

establishing shot: Synonymous with **master shot,** this is the shot generally photographed first to set the scene. Actors' movements and **dialogue** are fine-tuned at this stage, as is the **DP's** lighting plan. Afterward, it's on to the **close-ups,** termed **coverage.** "Movin' on!"

executive producer: The person responsible for providing the enormous sums of money needed for a film, either by putting up their own money or, better, getting the money from someone else, such as a studio, a bank, or a rich movie star like Demi Moore or Tom Cruise. This person will then share in any profit or loss, receive an executive producer **credit,** and get a flimsy **director's chair** with their name and the **working title** of the project on it.

expendables: These are the essential nonfood items purchased rather than rented by the **production manager** for the film, which are used up by the end of filming. Pens, **tape, gels**, wood, tape, **show cards, dulling spray, foam core**, tape . . . Movies go through cases of tape.

experimental films: These are arty short films safely made only within the walls of a film school, and are synonymous with noncommercial or "boring" films. Distinct from **documentaries** and **narrative** films, typical experimental titles might be *Colors of My Crayons* or *Nasty Papercut—Day 3*. Pass the LSD.

exposed: Film that has run through the camera is termed exposed, and is placed in light-tight **cans and bags**, and sealed with black tape. These cans are handled with care and guarded zealously, as a single can might represent the entire day's work for the **company**. At the end of the day, the precious cans of exposed film are handed to a minimum-wage low-level **PA** for the crosstown trip to the **lab**. Go figure.

exposure: This is an important technical term, but it's *not* the amount of positive or negative publicity a **star** garners. Simply put, the quantity of light hitting the film in the camera is your exposure. You can control it in any number of ways—by adding or subtracting lights on the **set**, by adjusting the camera **iris**, or by changing types of **raw stock** (film). Control of the exposure is critical to the final look of the film, and it is the sole province of the **DP**. That's why they get the big bucks.

exterior: Why can't movie people just say "outdoors" like the rest of the English-speaking population? Exterior (or EXT) on the schedule means "have warm clothing, sunscreen, and **rain gear** ready, because the **workday** will take place in the great outdoors." To complicate matters, the **screenplay** may indicate EXT (in story terms), but the shooting might take place on a giant indoor **sound-stage** filled with trees and dirt by the **greensman**.

extras: Actors who walk around but don't talk on screen. See **background**. Extras are recommended to the production by the casting agent. Pay is $115 per day, you provide your own transportation, and don't be surprised if you get sent to the back of the **catering** line at lunchtime, because "the **crew** eats first."

eyelight: A small light is sometimes placed just over the camera lens, in front of the actor (see also **obie**). This eight- to twelve-inch low-wattage white light source is reflected back to the film by the star's eyes. The eyelight travels along with the camera, so it's always there, improving our **thespian's** countenance.

eyeline: When you see your favorite **actors** on the big screen, it's easy to forget that once they were standing under movie lights,

facing a huge movie camera, with anywhere from four to forty people crowding around. Not an easy task, and in order to help them, it's best not to stand in their eyeline—the direction the actor is looking while filming. When filming a **close-up** of the co-star for the same **scene**, the **director** and **camera operator** will attempt to establish a complementary eyeline for this next **shot**, to aid **continuity**.

facade: A building or storefront can be created for filming by constructing only the front wall, the facade, and propping it up by temporary wooden supports and **sandbags**. Whole towns were made this way for popular Westerns such as *Rio Bravo* and *High Noon*. I visited the set of Mel Gibson's *Braveheart* in Ireland and was surprised to see the massive stone-and-earth buildings were actually constructed of lightweight vacuum-formed plastic. Well, at least it's recyclable!

fade out, fade to black: You know what this is: The image on the screen slowly changes to black. Roll **credits**!

false start: The **shot** being filmed starts poorly. The **dolly** gets bumped, the **actor** chokes on unfamiliar **dialogue**, or the **camera operator** makes an uncharacteristic mistake. You can **cut** the camera or muddle through the rest of the shot, but in any case the **script supervisor** notes it as a false start.

fast film: Kodak or Fuji film for the movie **camera** that is very sensitive to light is termed "fast." (It has a higher **ASA** or ISO rating.) Less light is needed to get a proper **exposure**, and it's great for shooting with **available light**.

feature: For Hollywood insiders, this is synonymous with a movie in production aiming for **theatrical distribution**, as opposed to a TV show, a **commercial**, an **industrial**, or a **PSA**. Features normally take longer to film than these other types of projects (four to twenty weeks) and are considered plum assignments. After all, you may get your name in the **credits**.

featured player: An **actor** with a little more time on the screen and more **lines** than a **bit player**, but not quite a supporting role or **leading man**. Sidekicks, **baddies,** and James Bond's girlfriends all fall into this category.

fill light: This is complementary to the **key light**, used to "fill" in the shadows created by the stronger key. Often fill lights are large, white, and diffuse, and placed near the camera position in front of the **actor**. As a generalization, comedies call for more and stronger fill lights than serious pieces, which might use deeper shadows for dramatic effect. Trade secret: Actresses can be made to look younger and more attractive by clever use of fill lights. See **obie**.

film noir: This is a French term literally meaning "black film," which denotes the hard-hitting themes and sordid subject matter, rather than any trouble with the film's **exposure**. Hard-boiled detective stories such as *Chinatown, The Big Sleep,* and, more recently, *L.A. Confidential* are examples of film noir.

film school: University-level critical study of the art of filmmaking. Schools with top reputations include USC, UCLA, NYU, Columbia, and Northwestern. Their approaches to the complex subject of filmmaking differ, but they all accept your money equally. College film-study programs provide a supportive environment, one where you are free to explore and make occasional mistakes without professional repercussions (such as getting **fired**). Do you need to go to film school in order to get a job on a movie shoot? I've never once been asked in twenty years where I went to school (Northwestern). If you do choose to spend the college fund on film school, make sure you go to one that lets you actually *make* films, not just talk about them.

film stage: See **soundstage**.

film stock: Not a gathering of cinema-loving hippies in upstate New York, film stock is synonymous with **raw stock**, film that has yet to be run through the **camera**. Movies generally keep fifteen thousand to fifty thousand feet of unexposed film on hand (90 feet = 1 minute of film), which is stored in **cans and bags** in a **darkroom** by the **loader**.

film-to-tape: Also called **video transfer**. The process by which the original film negative from the movie camera is transferred to digital videotape for viewing and editing. This generally happens daily during **principal photography**, with a fine-tuned and detailed film-to-tape transfer performed during **postproduction** once the editing has been completed. See **color correction**.

filter: One big difference between the person shooting home videos and the professional photographer (or cinematographer) is that the pro uses a lot more glass filters on the **lens** in front of the camera. It's not uncommon for the **AC** to carry around two heavy suitcases of specialized filters. If you've ever wondered why Los Angeles **productions** such as *L.A. Story* and *Training Day* look like they were filmed in two completely different Hollywoods, one small reason is creatively filtered light reaching the film through the lens. Three very common filters are **ND** (gray) to help control **exposure, 85** (orange) to balance the film's response to daylight, and **diffusion** to make the **star** look good.

final cut: This is what every **director** wants but very few achieve—that is, complete control over the ultimate form of the finished movie. Usually, final-cut privileges rest contractually with the **producer** or the **studio**. If you are one of the handful of directors with final-cut privileges (Spielberg, Bob Zemekis, Ron Howard), you've arrived, baby!

Final Cut Pro: Inexpensive editing software for **Apple** (Macintosh) computers, an alternative to **Avid** systems. You can edit your feature film, add music, toss in some pretty good special effects, all for about thirteen hundred dollars. Not bad. Countless lower-budget films and documentaries have used Final Cut Pro since its introduction in 1998. *Scrubs* in 2004 became the first prime-time TV show to edit and finish entirely with Final Cut software.

fire in the hole: When you hear this phrase, cover your ears and duck. This is the phrase **props** and pyrotechnical crews scream just prior to firing guns or blowing something up on **set**.

fired: Everyone who's worked on films for more than a few years has been invited to go home at one time or another. There are just too many clashing artistic egos, short-fused directors, and competing interests for the case to be otherwise. The people most likely to get the ax are the **AD** and the **DP**, generally when the **producer** needs a scapegoat for not shooting quickly enough. The **focus puller** occasionally gets canned if there is any type of camera malfunction or out-of-focus actors in the **dailies**.

first positions: This is the **mark** for the **actors** and **background** players at the beginning of the **shot**. Sometimes an **AD** will say, "Places!" or "**Back to one**" instead. Before filming can begin, everyone in the **cast** and **crew** needs to be ready at the same time, and it's the AD's job to get them there.

first shot: The exact time the **crew** executes the first **shot** each day is given great importance by the **producers** and **studio**. It is seen as an indicator of productivity. This first-shot time is written down for the **production report** and is telephoned in to the studio. Savvy **directors** will therefore simply turn on the camera first thing in the morning and photograph random **bogies**. First shot . . . 6:01 a.m.! That should get the suits off your back!

first team: When the **DP** is finished preparing the lighting (it could take minutes—or five hours) for a particular **shot**, he will inform the **AD**, who will in turn call for the first team (the lead actors) to come to **set**. They replace the second team (**stand-ins**), who've been patiently standing still on the **marks** in order to aid the lighting and camera crews.

fisheye lens: It's unclear how scientists know what a fish's field of vision is, but a very short **focal length** lens that provides a very wide, distorted image is called a fisheye.

fix it in the mix: When the film crew hurries through the day's work without taking the time and care to record a good-quality **soundtrack** of the actors' **dialogue**, they often delude themselves into thinking the editor can somehow salvage the soundtrack in the final editing process. See **ADR**.

flag: Another of the fundamental building blocks of professional filmmaking they never tell you about in **film school**. It's a black felt-covered metal frame used to reduce light and create shadows, sort of anti-lighting. They are generally held in place with a **gripstand**. The **electrics** point the lights, and the **grips** shape it with flags. Note, if the **DP** calls for a flag at the last minute to be handheld, it's referred to as a *Hollywood* by the NYC indie feature-film **crew**, but called a *hand-job* by the experienced **IA** (union) film workers. Nice.

flare: You know how difficult driving is when the sun is blasting directly into the windshield? Ever notice how clear and sharp your vision becomes outdoors when you don a baseball cap? You've shaded your eyes from **flare**, which is also the enemy of the movie camera **lens**. Great care is taken by the **grips** and the **AC** to shield the lens from all stray light sources. On the other hand, if you must shoot directly into the sun (as in a Warren Miller ski film), you should pretend the resulting flare is intentional and claim credit for it.

flashback: When the movie **plot** jumps back in time to the past, that's a flashback. Clichéd transitional devices employed by directors and editors to introduce flashbacks include wiggly lines, actor voice-over ("I remember July the ninth . . ."), and **black and white**. Woody Allen's best film, *Annie Hall,* was a dud with **preview** audiences until it was reedited by mixing in some flashbacks and breaking away from straight chronological order.

flicker: If your **dailies** flicker, generally this is a bad thing. Moving pictures should appear smooth and continuous without exhibiting any undue changes in **exposure**. Your eye's ability to process the twenty-four individual frames projected each second is termed **persistence of vision**. A little bit of each previous picture hangs over on your retina, and voilà! Movies! If you see nothing but flickering images in your **dailies,** you should (1) check the camera, (2) check the electrical **genny,** (3) check with your doctor.

flicks: Movies. Modern motion-picture **cameras** record twenty-four individual pictures each second, whereas early silent movies were filmed at eighteen frames per second, just below the average person's threshold for **persistence of vision.** They were also photographed with hand-cranked cameras (**camera operators** were termed *cranks*), contributing to the flickering effect.

fluid head: This is a type of **camera head,** the breadbox-size contraption mounted between the **dolly** and the **camera body,** and manipulated by the **camera operator** while filming to **frame** the **shots.** Quality heads are manufactured by Weaver, Ronford, and Sachtler, though I prefer the O'Connor 25-75B. See **kit rental.**

FO: This common saying is an abbreviation for "F%#* off," usually a request to remove (**strike**) something from the set, as in "FO that **grip stand,** please!"

foam core: This stuff is amazing. In everyday life, it's used to mount art pictures behind glass, to hold posters at trade shows, and to serve as a base layer for fiberglass boat building. On a movie **set** it can serve to redirect and soften light. The art department uses painted foam core for temporary **set pieces** and **teasers.** I like to make lightweight **sunshades** for the camera **lens** out of black foam core. Nothing like a one-dollar piece of foam paper protecting a ten-thousand-dollar **Primo** lens!

focal length: More math. Sorry. Focal length is specifically the distance (in millimeters) from the optical center of the **lens** to where the image is recorded (the film plane or video chip surface). This number can be an indicator of whether the lens will show a **panoramic** view or a **close-up**. A typical **telephoto** is 150 mm, whereas 25 mm is more of a **wide-angle**. Focal length is also an important variable when calculating **focus**. See **depth of field**.

focus: Selective focus is one of the filmmaker's artistic tools. Movie lenses have large focus rings that must be rotated during the shot to ensure sharp pictures of moving actors. See **focus puller**, **depth of field**. In the movie theater, a **projectionist** focuses the projector's lens by viewing the **academy leader** at the start of the film. During **editing**, a substandard **soundtrack** can be fixed with **ADR**, but bad focus in the **dailies** requires an expensive **reshoot**.

focus puller: 1st **AC** (assistant cameraperson). It takes two people to run a movie camera during a **shot**. The **operator** moves the **camera head** to point the thing (framing), and the focus puller controls all the **lens** functions, such as **zoom**, **aperture**, and **focus**. The camera crew directs the viewer's attention by coordinated subtle shifts of focus. Believe it or not, sharp focus is achieved by an experienced focus puller actually *guessing the distance* to the **actor** and twisting the lens barrel, without looking through the lens at the action! Moving **dollies** and improvising actors complicate things, and the assistant may refer to **marks** placed on the floor to aid him or her.

foley: Sound effects that are added long after the filming is over. Ironically, the movie crew works diligently to keep the shooting **set** quiet as a tomb during filming, and the first thing the **foley artist** does in **postproduction** is add back in all kinds of bird whistles, car door slams, footsteps, and so forth. Named for Jack Foley (1891–1967). Really.

foley artist: In the old days, this was the weird guy banging co-conut shells together to simulate pounding horse hooves in a small sound-recording studio months after the filming had finished. Today it's pretty much the same weirdo, except that he or she has access to dozens of prerecorded hoofbeats on a computer hard drive. I remember shooting William Hurt's Brooklyn apartment scenes on a quiet **soundstage** for the Miramax movie *Smoke*. The resulting **dailies** seemed totally artificial to me until months later, when I screened the finished film. Foley sound additions such as birdsongs, squealing tires, and gunshots blended into the background to make the pictures seem more realistic.

follow spot: This is a big powerful lamp used to throw a circle of bright light onto a performing stage from afar, like during a Broadway musical or a circus act (nearly the same thing these days). The follow spot is seldom used in movie production, because the intense beam looks *too* theatrical.

follow van: Crew members not riding on the **insert car** usually chase behind the driving movie **stars** and camera crew when filming **running shots** by riding in the follow van. This is normally packed with extra film **mags**, lenses, and makeup kits. Slight adjustments to the **setup** can be made roadside, though changes to costumes or lighting necessitate a trip back to **base camp**. See also **crew van**.

forced call: When the **crew** is requested (told) to return to work the next day on short **turnaround** (say, after four to five hours' rest), this is a forced call. The "invaded hours," time normally spent stuck in traffic or sleeping, are compensated at a much higher **rate** of pay. *Ka-ching!*

foreground: (1) **Action** given special prominence is said to be brought to the foreground.

(2) **ADs** will also use the term *foreground* to describe people in the scene walking between the main actors and the camera. When planned, this can lend a touch of realism to a crowd scene, if used sparingly. Too many **extras** all crowding around, trying to be Tom Cruise's best friend and to get their faces into the film, does not look good, however.

foreshadow: Filmmakers often drop hints along the way to introduce new **story points** and **themes** to the viewer. For instance, in Spielberg's *Jaws*—okay, it's my favorite film—Roy Scheider playing Chief Brody almost causes an accident by dropping a volatile air tank while loading Quint's boat. This foreshadows the film's ending, when Brody uses the tank to blow the shark to smithereens.

format: Examples of formats include 35 mm film, 16 mm film, super-16, Hi-Def video, VHS, DVD, Beta SP, miniDV . . . basically whatever type of tape or film is in your camera or recorder/player. Also see **aspect ratio**.

found location: As opposed to a movie **set** created from scratch, a found location is a suitable house, apartment, business, or building, where the movie **company** simply takes over. The **art department** may add or subtract a few items (curtains, pictures, and the like), but the major expense of set construction is avoided. Rental fees are negotiable.

four-banger: Nothing pornographic here, a four-banger is a large **trailer** with four doors housing dressing rooms, a production room, and a bathroom for the **crew**. For some reason, they seem to always have four doors. I've never seen a three-banger.

frame: (1) To "frame the **shot**" is a phrase meaning to choose the appropriate **lens** and position the **camera** accordingly. It's what the **camera operator** is paid to do, under the watchful eyes of the **DP** and the **director**. There were many fewer watchful eyes prior to the advent of **video assist**. Now everyone is a backseat driver. Can't they wait for **dailies**?

(2) As a piece of **grip** gear, a *frame* refers to a light metal structure that helps to control the light. Standard frames larger than a **flag** include 8 x 8 feet, 12 x 12 feet, and 20 x 20 feet (referred to as eight-bys, twelve-bys, twenty-bys).

freelance: Ever since the stranglehold on **cast, crew,** and **distribution** perpetuated by the Hollywood studio system ended in the wake of antitrust legislation in the 1950s, everyone basically works freelance, even Scorsese and Spielberg. **Stars** are no longer under onerous long-term contracts. Unlike baseball players. The USA has around 150,000 freelance movie crew people, all flowing between various projects. One week, you could be working on a hit film like *Chicago,* and the next on *Dude, Where's My Car?*

French flag: *Mon Dieu!* This refers to a small portable black **sunshade** attached in front of the camera in an attempt to reduce lens flare. It's unclear whether these are actually used on French movie productions, but it makes a nice shorthand name.

French hours: Another gift from the Gauls. *French hours* refers to the practice of working nine straight hours without a lunch break.

The producer provides a plate of cold sandwiches, and crews gobble them down while continuing to work. Not surprisingly, this arrangement is not very popular.

Fresnel: Pronounced *freh-nell*. Three definitions in a row for France! French designer and math whiz Augustin Fresnel (1788–1827) designed heavy, wavy, thick glass lenses shaped like concentric circles for the lighthouses along many of the world's coastlines. His designs are still in use today, and movie lights use Fresnel lenses to focus and concentrate the light beams.

front light: Often this is the **fill light**, which is a complement to the **key light**, and is placed facing the actors from near the camera position. A video news crew will use this as the only light, mounting a bright spotlight on top of the camera. Trade secret: **Soft lights** placed facing the actors from the front (camera position) can fill in the wrinkles and make older movie **stars** appear younger and more attractive.

front projection: Hard to believe, but once upon a time, there were no computers for **special effects**. Front projection is an old camera trick whereby the movie camera and a projector are wed  in an unholy union (using mirrors and precise alignment). The resulting shot superimposes **actors** onto a previously photographed background. We used a variation of this technique on Universal's *Virus*. A small light was mounted in place of the projector, with the light beam emanating from the exact position of the camera lens. The result—glowing, red-hot alien creatures.

f-stop: Those bizarre numbers on the **lens** have to mean something. In this case, the f-stop number refers to the size of the **aperture** (iris blades), which opens to allow light to reach the film. The f-stop setting is also one of the important variables when calculating **depth of field** and is set only by the **DP**, or by the **focus puller** under his direction. Hands off!

full load: (1) Camera-geek term for a camera **magazine** filled with a thousand feet of fresh film.

(2) Full load also refers to a **prop** gun loaded with maximum-size blanks. The guns shoot out a flaming paper-and-gunpowder wad that, though quite impressive-looking in a Vin Diesel action movie, is relatively safe to fire near innocent bystanders. I still have a small burn mark on my hand from a "movie gun." Camera crews normally hide behind Plexiglas or plywood shields.

full screen: This is when a **wide-screen** movie is reformatted by **pan and scan** to fit the almost square shape of the average home television. (See **aspect ratio**.) The use of the word *full* suggests "complete," but in this case, the sides have been cut off the original picture, and the viewer receives 30 percent less picture information than was in the original film. If you haven't seen *Lawrence of Arabia*, *Star Wars*, or *The Sound of Music* on the big screen, or at least on TV in **letterbox** form, you don't know what you're missing.

full shot: A camera angle that shows the **actor** from head to toe. Also cleverly called a head-to-toe. The early comedies of Buster Keaton and Charlie Chaplin unfold largely in full-length shots, which were perfectly suited to that type of broad comedy. Initially, when close-ups were introduced into films (about 1915), early audiences felt somehow cheated. "Hey, where's the *rest* of that guy!"

fuller's earth: Technically, this is magnesium aluminum silicate, used in everyday life as a soil conditioner, a grease absorber, and a pet litter. Movie **prop** people carry some in a sack and spread it around whenever a little extra dust in the air is needed. My own theory is that the United Artists feature *Heaven's Gate* flopped in 1980 because no one could see the actors riding around on horseback . . . too much fuller's earth swirling around!

furny pad: Hollywood term, short for *furniture pad*. East Coasters call them **sound blankets**. These are multipurpose quilted cotton coverings, normally hung about the **set** to reduce unwanted sounds. Of course, they can also be used as mattresses when sneaking a nap at lunchtime.

FX: Short for *EFX*, which is short for *effects*, which is short for *special effects*.

G

gaffer: Chief lighting technician. The origin of the term is a bit hazy, but it may derive from the early days of live theater, when lighting candles were snuffed out with long gaffs. Maybe. The gaffer is a visual stylist whose artistic medium is light rays in all types, shapes, and sizes—this in addition to being an electrician. He's the senior member of the **crew**, assisting the **DP** with creating beautiful lighting for the movie **stars**—what could be more important?

gaffer's tape: You call it duct tape. Movie gaffer tape is twice as expensive, half as sticky. Comes in gray and black.

gag: Any **stunt** or special-purpose device (**rig**) is termed a gag, whether or not there is any risk of choking. An **AD** might say, "We'll shoot the stagecoach-dragging-Madonna gag next!"

gear head: Large wheeled contraption that the **camera operator** manipulates to **frame** shots (aim the camera). The big wheel on the left side makes the camera go left and right; the one directly in front of the technician tilts the camera up and down. Camerapeople are experts at the child's game Etch A Sketch. The gear head is a design derived from early antiaircraft artillery. No joke. PanaHead, Arrihead, and Technohead are some popular types of gear heads, sometimes called *the wheels*. (See also **camera head**.)

gels: Large colored sheets of acetate (not actual gelatin) are placed in front of lights to flavor the resulting light beam, affixed with **C-47s** or mounted onto square frames. Gels come on forty-eight-inch-wide rolls and are cut to size for each application. Need a glowing moonlight effect? Try a **blue** gel in front of that **blonde**.

genny: Large trailer-mounted diesel-power generator. Movies use incredible amounts of electricity to provide power to the lights, trucks, and **trailers**, and **the company** usually travels with at least one large genny. Alternatively, the **gaffer** or trained **best boy** might **tie-in** to a building or house fuse box.

glycerin tears: Though some **actors** are able to cry on demand by thinking of their dead dog or something, the tears are indistinguishable from glycerin tears placed in the corner of the eye just prior to shooting by the makeup person. Hint: In the finished movie, if the actor goes from dry-eyed to bawling tears without a **cutaway** shot, the tears in the film are real.

go for me: This is the phrase an **AD** will say into a **walkie-talkie** instead of "Hello?"

go motion: Instead of the usual **stop-motion** animation techniques for photographing little spaceship models and the like, those whizzes at **ILM** (Industrial Light & Magic) have pioneered a method of using a little natural streaking and movement (previously considered mistakes) in their model photography. This helps give the illusion of motion and life to the **models**.

go to two: Walkie-talkie channel 1 is for the **AD** to bark orders, so all personal and juicy conversations are directed to switch to channel 2. Both involved parties will switch their walkies to channel 2 (as will eavesdroppers) to complete the conversation.

gobo: These are large adjustable four-inch aluminum knuckles permanently affixed to the end of **grip stands** that hold lights, **flags,** and so on, and look exactly like, well, Tinkertoys. Large metal tinkertoys. Gobo heads are deceptively difficult to manipulate with any sort of élan. For starters, remember "righty-tighty, lefty-loosey."

going again: After a completed **take,** the **director** will whisper to the **AD,** "That was perfect, let's do another take!" The AD resets the cast and crew by announcing, "Going again!"

Gone With the Wind: Producer David O. Selznick's 1939 film has worked its way into the lore and sayings of the modern film **crew.** "This ain't *Gone With the Wind* . . . hurry up, let's shoot!" or "Back when I was running **craft service** on *Gone With the Wind* . . ."

grad: Short for *graduated filter.* A glass **filter** placed in front of the **lens,** in which roughly half its surface area is clear and half is gray, red, or blue. These are used to control the **exposure** when photographing the sky, and when pressured by the producers to create an instant sunset shot.

Greek it out: This means to disguise the logo or label on a movie **prop.** It is likely that the product's manufacturer has been offered a **product placement** . . . for a fee, naturally. If the manufacturer doesn't pay up, the prop person will apply black paper tape to its logo or otherwise scribble on it to disguise the name. I'm not exactly sure why the process is named for the birthplace of Western democracy. Perhaps it's from the graphic artist term for unintelligible script. Whatever—it's Greek to me!

green room: This is another term from the Broadway theahhh-ter. The green room, which may or may not actually be painted green, is the backstage area where **actors** hang out, awaiting their turns on the stage. On movies, the **thespians** spend the time between shots chilling in their **trailers**.

green screen: Think about the TV studio weatherman standing in front of the camera, while all the squiggles and arrows of the weather map are superimposed behind him. The background is generated from another video source, and that's how modern **special effects** movies are made, as well. The *Spy Kids* movies were apparently made by Robert Rodriguez working alone with the actors in front of a big green screen. (He assigned himself **director**, **DP**, music, **screenwriter**, **production designer**, and **editor** credits.) All the **sets**, evil villains, backgrounds, and so forth were added later with computers. I guess we know whom to blame for *Spy Kids 3-D*, then.

greenlight: The pooh-bahs at the **studio** issue a greenlight when they have approved the intended film (A live-action *Scooby-Doo!?* Greenlight!) and are sending money. Once you get the greenlight, movie **stars**, **Panavision** cameras, and the **freelance** film crew will follow within a few weeks.

greensman: Standard part of a Hollywood **crew**, the greensman is responsible for artfully arranging plants, flowers, and trees for each shot. Think of it as instant landscaping. Greenery is often used to disguise movie equipment such as lights, **cables,** and even **trucks** from the camera lens.

grid: On a **soundstage,** pipes and lumber are hoisted overhead to support lights, cables, scenery, and the like. Sitcoms and weekly TV shows often utilize lights preplaced on the grid or up in the **perms,** and this is one reason they look a little different from Hollywood features. Films use lights on stands placed individually for each **shot.**

grip: How to describe this essential and unique individual? These riggers are the backbone of the film **shoot.** They set **flags** in front of lights, they move the camera on **dollies** and **track,** they erect the sets—I've even seen them help a child actor hold up an ice cream cone by creating a cleverly hidden armrest. Whatever needs doing, the grips are there to help. That's one problem with making short films in a university **film school:** too many directors-in-training and not enough grips.

grip stand: Along with **apple boxes, show cards,** and lights, grip stands (sometimes called **C-stands**) are one of the most important filmmaking tools. A movie might carry forty grip stands to support all the lights, flags, video monitors . . . well, just about anything on the **set.** Note: Productions shooting in third world countries such as India and China often employ humans to hold up all the equipment. Labor costs are cheaper than gear rentals. No kidding.

Groucho: The funniest Marx brother, also the name given an advanced film-acting trick. To stay in the view of the camera by crouching is a Groucho. Minus the cigar and mustache, of course.

grown-up: Slang for someone with real decision-making authority, such as the **director, producer,** or the **DP**. "Dave, should we shoot an **establishing shot** before the **close-ups**?" Ask a grown-up.

guide track: When the **soundtrack** recorded live by the **mixer** is ruined by noise beyond their control (such as a nearby train track or construction site), he or she will settle in exasperation for a simple guide track, a flawed recording of the **dialogue**. The director, editor, and the actors use this later during **ADR**.

guild: Any time a union wants to dress up its image a bit, it simply changes its name and becomes a guild. The Directors Guild, the Writers Guild, and the International Cinematographers Guild are three examples of organizations of film workers that function as unions.

hack: Term of derogation, a hackney, a filmmaker lacking in the subtleties of style and imagination. Delivering a completed film on a tight **shooting schedule** can certainly lead one to hack away at the day's work.

hair: The difference between Sean Connery the actor and James Bond. Also: a small piece of loose film **emulsion** finding its way just behind the lens, casting an unwanted image onto the film—a bad thing. See **check the gate.**

hair and makeup: Movie **stars** need to look good, and each one has an assigned **makeup artist** and a **hairdresser.** The talented makeup artist can beautify the star's face and erase years of hard living. To maintain consistency over the course of a ten-week shoot, an actor's hair will need to be unnoticeably trimmed, and before every shot, the hairdresser checks not only that the star looks good, but also that the hairstyle matches from **take** to take.

haircut: Apparently when the **camera operator** makes an error and the resulting **shot** is too low, the actor's head partially leaves the **frame.** This is referred to as a haircut, a mistake that is quickly brought to the operator's attention by the helpful citizens of **video village.** Then the shot is redone. Hey, nobody's perfect!

half apple: Three-inch-thick black wooden plywood box, the smaller brother to the **apple box**.

hammer: This is archaic slang for a **grip**, as today's film worker is more likely to work with a metal **speed rail** and cordless drills than the traditional wooden platforms, hammers, and nails.

hamper: Workers in the **electric** and **prop departments** move their gear around in large rolling hampers, such as those used by industrial launderers. Changing the camera angle initiates a dance of moving cameras, lights, and hampers. Prop hampers generally have locks, as valuable items such as watches, jewelry, and guns used for filming need to be strictly accounted for.

handheld: The movie camera is simply placed on the **camera operator's** shoulder, rather than on a **dolly** or **sticks**. A favorite technique of poor film students, documentarians, and weird Danish directors, handheld is sometimes seen as more "real" than other styles of shooting. This is because of the traditions of war reportage, where the smallest cameras possible are used out of necessity. Handheld in big **Hollywood** movies is often used for fight scenes and in places where one wants to artificially create some excitement (for example, *The Blair Witch Project*). **Steadicam** is another way to go.

hardlight: Light coming directly from a movie lamp or the sun, uninterrupted by a net or a soft **bounce**. Old **Hollywood** movies used a lot of large directional hardlights, as film **emulsion** in those days wasn't very sensitive. The **crews** were masters at shaping and balancing beastly large lamps drawing thousands of kilowatts of electricity. The effect on the screen, however, can be quite subtle—just dig the great atmosphere created on classics such as *Casablanca* or *Out of the Past*.

hazard pay: Sometimes when working around helicopters, water, charging buffalos, and the like, the movie **crew** might politely ask Mr. Producer for an extra hundred dollars each, a hazard **bump**. *Ka-ching!*

headroom: (1) The amount of space between an actor's hair and the top of the **frame** as seen by the movie camera. Compared with home videos—in which the amateur cameraman often places the person's head floating squarely in the middle of the picture—**Hollywood** films leave little or no space above the actor's head on **close-ups**.

(2) In audio recording, the amount of reserve volume before the sounds overpower the tape or digital recorder, causing distortion.

headshot: Every **actor** and aspiring actor (waiter) has one. These are personal eight-by-ten-inch black-and-white close-up photos with a résumé stapled to the reverse side. **Casting agents** and **producers** collect piles of headshots, whole books of them, and  during production of a film, the headshots of the lead actors are taped to the wall of the production **office** like trophies.

hero: (1) A grinder or submarine sandwich, the kind eaten by the film crew when working **French hours**.

(2) The **leading man** starring in the film.

(3) *Hero* is also the term given any special **prop** or accessory, as in "Gimme the hero bomb, we're shooting a close-up!" This is a request from the **prop master** for the best-looking bomb from his no-doubt extensive collection of these props. In **master shots**, the actor will run around with a fake plastic bomb, and for the effects shots you'll need to substitute an actual explosive device, but the close-up—that calls for the hero bomb. Cut the blue wire!

hi boy: This is a really big **grip stand**, a veritable **C-stand** on steroids. Used in tandem for flying large **silks** overhead, this reduces the harsh direct sunlight and makes actors and actresses look nice for **close-ups**.

hi hat: A camera tripod with its legs cut off, affixed to an eighteen-inch square of three-quarter-inch plywood. The resulting metal camera-mounting device is four inches tall and resembles Abe Lincoln's trademark stovepipe hat.

hi roller: Not some Vegas character played by Joe Pesci, a hi roller is a **hi boy** with wheels. These can be handy for adjusting large **flags** and lights—just watch that a gust of wind doesn't turn it into a land-based windsurfer.

highlight: A slash of bright light striking just one part of a **shot** is termed a highlight if placed there intentionally by a master **DP**, such as Gordon Willis or Conrad Hall. However, if a clown like me lets a blast of unintentional light hit the **actors**, it's a mistake, termed a **flare**.

hit the mark: Something of a lost art in the world of reality-based TV and documentary-style features, *hit the mark* refers to the ability of an **actor** to stop at a fairly exact point on the floor. Without limiting movement too much, the goal is for them to stop or pause at previously agreed-upon points (without looking down!). This makes it possible for the **DP** to light them, the **focus puller** to keep them sharp, and the **camera operator** to include them in the movie.

HMI: Hydragyrum medium arc-length iodide, of course! Math and chemistry—this moviemaking is harder than it looks, folks. *HMI* refers to a very popular type of AC (normal electricity)-powered **arc**

lamp. Actually powerful enough to counterbalance sunlight, HMIs produce a lot of light from relatively little electrical current, and don't create much heat. They've pretty much replaced the old Hollywood DC arc lights.

hold the roll: On **set**, the **AD** will say, "Hold the roll" to suspend the start of a **shot** briefly, due to some unforeseen last-minute change. When the problem is resolved, it's time to **"Roll sound!"**

holding area: Extras and people not directly involved with setting up lights and cameras just get in the way of the working crew, and they are corralled in the holding area—a large space nearby rented for this purpose, such as a church or school basement. When needed, they are summoned to the set via **walkie** by the **AD**. "Bring me twenty tattooed teenagers on skateboards, *now!*"

Hollywood: The center of it all, ground zero for the movie business. Tinseltown. The neighborhood located roughly

between Beverly Hills and Griffith Park. And a hell of a hard place to find a parking spot.

Hollywood stand-up: This term has nothing to do with comedy or the Laugh Factory. A Hollywood stand-up refers to an acting technique whereby the **actor** in a film rises from a chair a little more slowly than usual. This gives the **camera operator**, who has hundreds of pounds of camera gear to manipulate, a good chance at following the action and keeping the actor in **frame**. For an excellent description of this and other great film-acting techniques, see Michael Caine's book *Acting in Film*.

home theater: Today's film fans want to bring all the excitement of **Hollywood** home with them. (They obviously haven't driven  through downtown Hollywood in the middle of the night lately.) For home theaters, better speakers and sound systems contribute greatly to the experience, and larger home TV screens showing **letterbox** widescreen presentations more closely resemble the original **theatrical release**. Pass the popcorn!

honeywagon: The **trailer** holding the portable toilet for use by the **crew**, so called because of the wonderful odor emanating from within.

hostess tray: This piece of **grip** equipment is used for **car rigs**. It is a camera mount on a flat tray attached to a car door, much the same way the food was served at old drive-ins, such as Mel's Diner or A&W.

hot brick: Not some esoteric Thai massage technique, a hot brick is **AD**-speak for a fresh **walkie** battery.

hot head: This is a type of camera system operated by remote control while staring at a video screen and working two control wheels or a joystick. It's a lot like playing a video game and getting paid for it. Often used for filming **stunts** or high angles while placed on a **crane**. Other types of **remote heads** include the Power Pod, Technocrane, Matthews Cam-Remote, and the Louma Crane.

hot points: Same as "Watch your back!" This is what a **crew** person says while charging through a crowded **set** with a large spearlike **tripod** in hand.

hot set: Once the first complete **master shot** is **in the can,** everything within view is considered "hot." Nothing can be altered or rearranged without affecting the **continuity** of future shots. It's important not to move the furniture, to change anything, or to secretly eat the prop food from the dinner table scene. Head for **craft service** instead.

house: (1) The attendance, or the part of a Broadway theater with the seats. "How's the house tonight? Almost empty! Everyone's at the movies!"

(2) On a movie **set,** *house* refers to items belonging to the resident building or **soundstage,** as opposed to items belonging to **the company** loaded in from the **prop** truck.

house power: Drawing electricity from the residence or **soundstage,** as opposed to a **genny.** See **tie-in.**

houselights: The first order of business when setting up lighting for a movie is to **kill** the houselights (any resident lamps, overhead fixtures, and so forth). Next, the **electric** crew spends two hours dragging in their own bigger, better, more expensive **movie lights.** Our **stars** are worth it!

hubble: (1) A really big outer space telescope named after the famous scientist, lawyer, and Spanish-language teacher Edwin Hubble.

(2) A common type of electrical plug found on movie **sets,** but no relation.

IA: The IA, short for the International Alliance of Theatrical Stage Employees and Motion Picture Machine Operators of the United States and Canada. Whew! This is the **union** covering all film camerapeople, **electrics**, **grips**, costumers, sound **mixers**, and the like. Roughly half the movies shot in the USA do so under the union banner. With about a hundred thousand members, the IA ensures safety, administers the health and retirement plans, and negotiates contracts to represent **crews**. Hey, if you're one of the many Americans who for some reason are anti-union on principle, let me remind you that labor unions invented *the weekend*. That's right, baby, believe it! But if you'd rather work six twelve-hour days in a sweatshop every week . . . Wait a minute, that sounds like my job working on movie **sets**!

ILM: Industrial Light & Magic is George Lucas's gazillion-dollar company, created from the swirling vortex of the first three *Star Wars* films. ILM today creates many of the best **visual effects** around, either à la carte for movies needing a couple of trick **shots**, or for whole films. Whether using models or computers, twenty-five years later, ILM is still the benchmark for high-quality effects. Whether Yoda is a puppet or a pixel, he's still that old lovable green slimy guy. ILM's more than one hundred feature film credits include *The Mummy, The Perfect Storm, Jurassic Park, Harry Potter and the Sorcerer's Stone,* and *Master and Commander.*

improv: Improvisation. Making up the **dialogue** and **action** without prior **rehearsal**. Often used by **actors** exploring their characters while preparing for a movie, after which they are politely asked by the **director** to deliver the **lines** as scripted.

in the can: (1) When the intended **shot** or **scene** is completed to everyone's satisfaction, it is said to be in the can. The completed film in question is literally placed in a tin can by the **loader** for transport to the **lab**.

(2) In a larger sense, a film that has completed **principal photography** is said to be in the can.

independent film: This was once the term for any feature film made outside the studio system, away from Hollywood's control, such as *Easy Rider, Eraserhead,* or *Sex, Lies, and Videotape.* These days, there has been a splintering of **studios**, with each of the giant corporations (Sony, Disney, Steven Spielberg) having their own "independent" mini-studios cranking out dozens of studio-approved smaller films each year. The new, true independent is anyone with three thousand dollars, a video camera, and an Apple iMac. Taking filmmaking to the streets—let's go!

indie: Independent film, see above.

industrial: Films or videos made in-house for large corporations are termed industrials. The subject matter can be anything from *Our New Widget!* to *Fashion Week at Dior . . . Panic and Paisley!*

inky: Small—I mean *really* small, tiny in fact—movie lamps generally brought onto the **set** at the last minute to create a **dingle** of light, highlight a potted plant, or cast a heavenly glow on an actor's hair.

insert: Generally, the **close-up** shots of TV sets, clocks, guns, and the like are filmed after the important shots are completed, and the highly paid movie **stars** go home. Inserts help tell the story of the film by providing new information and by bridging unrelated **shots**. These can be a godsend to a harried **editor**.

insert trailer, insert car: Crews go to great lengths to photograph movies on the road. When filming cars, it's difficult to control the lighting and sound quality, and it's unbelievably time consuming. That's why in TV movies with limited budgets, the **actors** generally just sit and talk rather than drive cars. If driving is essential, the crew may employ **poor man's process** or use an insert trailer. To wit—the **hero** car is put on a low trailer and towed. **Cameras** and lights are rigged on the car, and the crew piles on the back of a tow truck that's festooned with video monitors, **cables**, lights, spare batteries, lenses, and the rest. In 1992, we fell behind schedule on *Scent of a Woman,* so to expedite things, the crew rigged six huge **Panavision** cameras surrounding Al Pacino and Chris O'Donnell while "driving" a Ferrari. Overflow **crew** people and equipment travel behind in a **follow van**.

insurance day: If an additional day of shooting is needed to accommodate a **lab** mistake, a sick movie **star**, or other unforeseen act of God, the **producer** will ask the insurance company to fund an extra day of work. Bad weather, an inebriated actor forgetting his lines, or just plain old lousy photography are *not* reasons that qualify for an insurance day. Sorry.

interior: Regular people call it "indoors." A **set** where you create your own lighting, and you most likely won't get rained on, abbreviated INT. This can be a **practical location** or a set built on a **soundstage**.

inverse square law: This is an easy and important rule of physics that every **grip, gaffer, electric,** and **DP** knows by heart. The amount of light coming from any light source varies according to the *square of the distance* from that source. If you move a lamp twice as far away from the actor, you'll get one-quarter the intensity. It's on the test, in case you want a **union** card. Clearly, how far away you place a movie light is an important variable.

iPod: Director Peter Jackson reportedly used these mini computer hard drives to transport the digital video **dailies** to and from the **set** of the *Lord of the Rings* movies. And they play music, too.

iris: The **aperture** inside the **lens** through which light passes on the way to becoming indelible movie images. The iris ring surrounding the lens is adjusted by the camera crew for each individual **shot** as a way to control **exposure**.

Jack Lord: A fine TV actor, but also popular movie slang for a 50 mm **lens**. Whenever legendary **AC** Vinnie Gerardo *(Sophie's Choice, Hair, Kramer vs. Kramer)* wanted to switch to a 50 mm lens, he would announce "Jack Lord!" (50 mm, five-zero, Hawaii 5-o, Jack Lord . . . get it?) Here's a great example of an industry professional disguising his meaning from the casual listener. Other popular and entertaining terms people use for a 50 mm lens include: Two inch! The deuce! Half a **buck**!

jib: The foremost sail on any sailboat, sure, but jib also refers to an articulated arm supporting a movie camera. These are similar to the larger **crane,** but the smaller jib would have a hard time supporting a full-figured cameraperson in addition to the camera.

John Ford: One of the greatest American **directors**. If you truly want to learn filmmaking, stop reading this book right now and head for the video store to rent his fantastic film *The Searchers*! A *John Ford* is also the name given a very stylish technique in which an **actor** walks forward toward the camera (**downstage**) in the course of a long take, eliminating the need for additional shots, because he's walked into his own close-up.

K: In banking, real estate, and producing, this is short for one thousand American dollars, but in the workaday world of the movie **set**, it's short for one thousand *watts*. Therefore, a 10K is a tenthousand-watt lamp, a 2K is a two-thousand-watter, and so on. Most electrical things are referred to in K, in order to ensure safety and to avoid blowing fuses. Even if they flunked algebra in high school, every man or woman on a movie's **electric** crew knows Ohm's law (watts = amperes X volts). Now you know it, too. Impress your friends.

key grip: George C. Scott once said in an interview that if stranded on a desert island what he would most desire is food, shelter, and a **grip**. The key (most important) **grip** is head of the grip department (two to ten people) and is responsible for safety on the movie set, among other things. He oversees the use of all lifts, **parallels**, and **rigs**. Grips (particularly the **dolly grip**) also move the camera by means of **dollies**, **jibs**, and **cranes**. The key grip is the go-to leader on the **set**, the one person who answers questions such as "Can we turn this set into a night scene?" or "How the heck are we going to **shoot** this shot?"

key hair: This is the person in charge of cutting, brushing, and maintaining the locks of the lead actor and actress. **Stars** and hairdressers often develop a mutually dependent relationship, with the key hair keeping the star looking good for the cameras, and the star hiring them for the **next big one**.

key light: The main source of illumination for a scene is the key light, and it can be the sun, a movie light, or a **reflector** board. Not necessarily coming from in front of the actor, often the key light is placed to the side or even behind an actor for dramatic effect. The lighting crew maintains the predominant direction of the key light when changing **shots**; this helps to establish good **continuity**.

key makeup: It takes many people and some tricky application of proprietary beauty products to transform an **actor** into a movie **star**, and the person in charge of this process is the key makeup.

kicker: A light generally placed at the last minute from behind or the side of the subject, in order to provide a **highlight**—to an actor's hair, for instance. Kickers and **rimlights** help provide visual separation between foreground and background elements within a **shot**.

kill: To stop, to eliminate, to cease to exist. Kill is **electric** department shorthand for "turn off" or "unplug." Kill the **blonde**!

Kino: Kinoflos (pronounced *kee-no-flow*) are fluorescent light fixtures made for movies, but without the usual noisy hum and green color light beam. Since they're "movie" lights, they cost ten times more than they're worth, like NASA equipment. Kinos have become wildly popular on all types of **shoots**. The light they give off is pleasing, and the units will fit into tight spaces.

kit rental: Personal equipment that **crew** people rent to the stingy producer to augment their incomes. Cameras, pickup trucks, **filters**, lights, and hammers are all potential kit rental items.

klieg lights: Let's get rid of this term once and for all. This is a brand of old-fashioned **Hollywood studio** spotlight not used in films since the 1940s, but for some reason, movie critics always refer to the hot "klieg lights" illuminating the **stars** on movie sets. The  high-power **arc** lamps developed by the brothers Kliegl in Hollywood are occasionally used to sweep the sky for gala events, such as mall openings (Yeah! A new mall!), but if you actually pointed a klieg light at someone, you'd melt his or her face.

kraft paper: Huge four-foot-wide rolls of plain brown wrapping paper are rolled out on the floors and taped to the walls by the location manager in an effort to appease owners of nice **practical locations**. Dozens of muddy-boot-wearing crew people carrying heavy equipment are on the way, and they can easily wreak havoc on nice floors or antique carpets. The protective paper is removed from the parts of the floor in view of the camera, just prior to shooting.

lab: Where the film gets developed. Film from the movie camera is dunked in various "soups" of harsh chemicals, dried off, and returned to the production the next day. Labs generally have screening rooms for viewing these **dailies** (or rushes), as well as offering services like 16 mm film processing, **film-to-tape** transfer, and release printing.

lamp operator: This is a midlevel **electric** who operates a particular movie light, often mounted high up on **parallels** or a **snorkel lift**. Consistency in lighting is important to the **DP**, so a lamp operator might remain up there for several hours at a time, without a bathroom break.

lap dissolve: See **dissolve**. So called because one shot in the final film briefly overlaps the other. The **editor** uses this technique to allow a smooth transition between **shots** or **scenes**.

last looks: Before the **AD** calls **"Roll sound!"** they will announce "Last looks!" The **hair and makeup** people scurry in and quickly **touch up** the movie stars and check for any mismatches in **continuity** or pieces of lettuce between teeth.

latitude: The ability of a particular type of film to successfully photograph both bright **highlights** and dark shadows. In general, film has much wider latitude than video (for the moment). It can capture a wider range of tones. One reason *The Sopranos* looks better than a daytime soap is that it's shot on film.

lav: Not the lavatory. This is short for *lavalier,* a type of small **mic** placed on an actor's lapel, such as those worn by sports- and newscasters. On a movie, they're hidden under clothing. Sportscasters have the luxury of having wires draped all over the place, and often use those curly white wires sticking out of their ears. They don't even try to disguise them, unlike Marlon Brando's **earbud.**

lavender: Somewhat of a rarity on the **set** these days, a lavender is a very thin, light purple fabric **net** that is rigged by the **grips** much the same as a conventional net or a silk. One uses them to subtly filter the light beam from a **hardlight.** "Put a lavender on the **redhead!**"

lead man: Not an **actor** at all. The lead man is the assistant set decorator, who leads a mad scramble to find, rent, or steal the essential **props** necessary for filming.

leading man: This is the main **actor.** Harrison Ford, John Wayne, or if you're younger, Vin Diesel, Brad Pitt. You know the type. The handsome young actor who gets the girl at the end of the film. Credit goes to Dustin Hoffman for being the first unconventional leading man in Hollywood for his role in *The Graduate.* Now we have lots of unconventional leading men, like Adam Sandler, Macaulay Culkin, and . . . Hilary Swank.

legs: (1) When a film's **theatrical release** lasts well past the opening **weekend** into a second or third or fourth week, it's said to have legs.

(2) On **set** the word *legs* refers to a camera support **tripod**. These come in regular, baby, and **hi hat** sizes, depending on how tall you want to set the **shot**. The **AC** normally attends to all the camera gear, but in this case, a **grip** might aid in the tripod setup. "Bring me the **brownie** on a **hi hat**!"

lens: Pieces of glass in a tube through which light rays stream, recording the scene onto film. Good-quality lenses are made for movie cameras by Angenieux (French), Zeiss (German), Cooke (English), and Leitz (German-Canadian). They can cost up to thirty thousand dollars each, so don't drop one! Hold on to the lens with both hands, and shuffle your feet across the **set**. No running.

letterbox: Movies on DVD and VHS are often presented in either **full-screen** or letterbox **wide-screen** versions. Some people feel ripped-off when the letterbox blacks out the top and bottom of the picture, but the fact is, you're seeing the same **aspect ratio** as the original **theatrical release** of the film. The image framed the way God and your **camera operator** intended.

LFS: Hardworking movie **crews** generally shoot ten to thirty individual **shots** in one day, and the LFS is the much-anticipated last f%#*ing shot of the day.

light meter: This is the totem object, an article of great importance for the **DP**, the chief of the movie **crew**. Light meters measure the exact amount of light falling on our beloved movie stars, and aid the DP and **gaffer** in determining **exposure** and setting the lights.

lighting cameraman: British way of describing the **DP**, or cinematographer. In England, the DP specifically takes charge of lighting the **set**, and the **camera operator** works closely with the **director** and **actors**, figuring out the **blocking** and camera placement.

limbo: In the Broadway theater, *limbo* refers to a set painted black without furniture or props. In movies, the limbo effect is achieved by lighting only the **actor**, and not the walls. A **scene** presenting an actor "in limbo" highlights his individuality, loneliness, or despair, one man against the world. That sort of thing.

line: (1) One or two sentences of scripted **dialogue**, spoken by an **actor** in turn. During a **rehearsal**, a forgetful **thespian** might loudly call "Line!" to elicit prompting help from the **script supervisor**.

(2) The term *line* is also used by the sound **mixer** and the **electrics**, in which case, it's short for *cable*.

line of force: See also **cross the line** and **screen direction**. It takes all three definitions to explain what is basically one complicated but important concept. Viewers are disoriented if presented with a fractured reality; we need to help them, the poor dears. If two Western gunmen face off on a dusty street, an imaginary line of force is created between them. As **director**, you need to plan your shots so that one guy always faces *left* when seen by the camera, and the other guy faces *right*. You *can't cross the street* and do a shot from the other side. The NFL labels these "reverse angles" so as not to disorient beer-guzzling viewers, but alas, feature film directors aren't afforded that luxury.

line producer: The line producer is the only one of the group of many **producers** who is actually working alongside the **crew,** making the movie on a daily basis. They function as a sort of super-**production manager.** The other producers can be found drinking Starbucks coffee and making cell phone calls from their **director's chairs** in **video village.**

line-up: During a line-up on set, in this sense a skeletal first rehearsal, the **DP** places the camera and the **actors** practice their movements. "Useful suggestions" or changes are made to the **scene** at this point. The rest of the **crew** watches attentively and plans how to film the scene once the actors go **in the works.**

live action: This is a term often used to describe movies that film with real people as **actors.** Whereas **animation** images are created slowly and painstakingly, a live-action shoot is where something *alive* is moving around, and you shoot it (with cameras).

load-in: Hours before the **director** and movie **stars** arrive for the day, the **grip, electric, prop,** and camera **crews** have unloaded the equipment trucks and schlepped a mountain of moviemaking machinery into place for the filming. This process is the load-in. After a twelve-hour workday, it's time to load out.

loader: Additional assistant in the **camera department** who puts the film in the **mags,** keeps the camera reports, and fetches a cup of tea, if the **camera operator** asks nicely. Called the clapper/loader in England, as one of their functions is to clap the **slate,** marking a sync point for the picture and sound.

location: Place where the movie magic is going to take place for the day. This can refer in general terms to a city, or specifically to a particular apartment, building, or even a street corner. By the way, if you've ever considered letting a movie **company** use your home for a location (Oh boy! Hollywood!), just imagine sixty strangers walking through your living room in muddy boots on their way to use your only bathroom.

location fee: This is a bribe—oops, an honorarium—paid to the owner of a **practical location**. This could be thousands of dollars or just fifty bucks, depending on the budget of the film and how badly the **producer** wants to use that location in the movie.

location manager: The liaison between the working **crew** and the owners of the **location** in which filming takes place. If the **electrics** need to put a light on the rooftop, the location manager is there. If the **art director** needs the apartment owner's ugly oil painting removed, the location manager is there. If the **DP** arrives late and hurries across the room, spilling his coffee all over an oriental rug, the location manager is there.

location scout: One of my early jobs was as a location scout for a fake bacon product **commercial**, and I really enjoyed myself. I drove around the countryside as fast as I could, taking as many **Polaroid** pictures of farms as possible. I reported only to the commercial's **director**. I felt like a king. When I suggested to the **client** they rename the product "Fake-on," we had "creative differences," and I went home. Today's specialized scouts have files on all kinds of places suitable for filming. Need a cheap rental on a friendly baseball park? Need an abandoned warehouse facing west near a mountain? A location scout can find it for you.

lock it up: When the **AD** announces this phrase over the **walkie**, filming is imminent. **PAs** gently encourage those not essential to working the **shot** to *stand still and be quiet!* Nearby whispers will be picked up by the sensitive **mics,** and moving bodies can distract the **actors.** See **eyeline.**

lockup: Your particular lockup means your "battle station" during filming if you're a **PA.** Also describes the process by which **bogies** are kept from inadvertently walking in front of the camera. Film **crews** will resort to any means necessary to clear the streets of noncombatants, especially during **stunts.** Lying to passersby is encouraged. "It's an insecticide commercial—no movie stars!"

lookie-loo: Gawking passersby who might potentially ruin the **shot** being filmed are termed lookie-loos. The **AD** sends over a polite **PA** to try to convince them to move along . . . or at least to stand *behind* the camera.

looping: See **ADR.** The process by which an actor's **dialogue** is replaced during **postproduction.**

losing the light, people: A popular motivational phrase, normally screamed by the panicked **AD** at sunset, when he or she real-izes the **shooting schedule** calls for an impossible number of daylight **shots** before **wrap.** As the saying goes, "Time and tide wait for no man." I'm not sure about tide, but I know when the sun is setting on a Hollywood film **crew—clear!** (That is, stand aside.) At these times the crew works like crazy, and all pretense of "art" or "good photography" goes right out the window.

low boy: A twelve-inch support stand for lights and grip equipment, the opposite of the **hi boy**. Lights set low on the floor of the **set** can serve to create extreme shadows and to trip up inattentive **actors**.

lunch: The company works six hours and then breaks for a hot lunch when the **AD** calls, "That's lunch, one-half!" Food is provided in **catering**, and the half-hour meal period starts with the last person to go through the line. If you run to the front of the line, your lunch period can be extended by about fifteen minutes . . . time enough for dessert, or a quick nap! By the way, after lunch, get ready to buckle down, because movies typically shoot for another six hours before **wrap**.

lunch box: No food involved, *lunch box* is slang for a portable electrical power distribution box, which resembles, well, a gray lunch box. A larger version that you might find on a **soundstage** is the **stagebox**.

MacGuffin: This term is used only by know-it-all academic film critics and film students majoring in Alfred Hitchcock studies. *MacGuffin* refers to an item or idea that serves as the motivating force for the film's characters, and around which the **plot** turns. The classic example is the statue in *The Maltese Falcon*. It doesn't really matter that the bird is a fake in the end—oops, hope I didn't ruin the ending for anybody!—it has served its purpose in driving along the plot.

macro: Modern movie **lenses** normally can **focus** only on objects two feet away and farther. A macro lens is one with the special ability to focus up close on small (micro) objects, like postage stamps, typewritten words, eyeballs. I mention eyeballs because I was credited as Eyeball Director of Photography for my macro photography in the title sequence of the film *Double Whammy*. Best part of the film, if you ask me.

mafer: (Pronounced *maff-er*.) Small strong clamps used by **grips** for mounting stuff, though less popular these days than the ubiquitous **cardellini** clamp. In a pinch, a mafer clamp can also be used to open cold malty adult beverages at **wrap**.

mag stripe: One of the several ways a soundtrack can be married to the picture in a finished **release print** is to add the audio information physically to the film on a stripe of magnetic audiotape. The resulting stripe of audiotape, as well as this sandwich of film and tape, is referred to as *mag stripe*.

magazine, mag: Interchangeable light-tight boxes clamp onto the 35 mm film **camera body** and hold the film. Unexposed film is in one compartment, and after it passes through the camera guts, exposed film winds up in another. **ACs** place the mags in heavy cases and shuttle them back and forth between the **darkroom** and the **set** in a continuous moving ballet. The mags are covered with lots of brightly colored **tape,** indicating the film's status, type, date, and **roll** number.

magic hour: Not to be confused with happy hour. The time after sunset when there is still some ambient light in the sky and everything turns lovely shades of orange and pink (see the great film *Days of Heaven,* photographed by **Oscar** winner Néstor Almendros). Once the sun begins to go down, the rush is on to shoot as many **shots** as quickly as possible. You may have more than an hour if you're in Sweden above the arctic circle in the summer, but what are the odds of that?

main title credit: The people listed on the screen individually before the film starts are big shots: **director, producer,** movie **stars,** and so forth. These are coincidentally also the folks on **set** who have a **director's chair** with their name on it. Everyone else on the **crew** settles for a **credit** listed after the film and, on set, a wooden **apple box** to sit on. Watch for splinters . . . you know where.

make the day, make the schedule: When all the scheduled daily **shots** are completed on time, you've made your day. If you finish the project without additional unplanned shooting days, you've made the schedule. The film might look terrible and the **plot** might be an incoherent mess—but hey, we finished on time!

man-maker: A pile of **apple boxes** on which a short actor stands in order to appear as tall as the co-star. Let's just say some big **stars** aren't quite as tall as you might expect, based on a viewing of their films. Does this qualify as naughty gossip? Oh, I can't help myself: Tom Cruise, Salma Hayek, and Sylvester Stallone (yo!) are three stars who might be candidates for some vertical assistance.

mark: Bits of **tape**, chalk lines, sandbags, or even golf tees are scattered about the floor of the **set** as reference marks for the **focus puller,** who measures distances to the camera with a tape measure. Hopefully the **actors** will move in a predictable manner, the focus puller adjusts the **lens** during the **shot**, and the actor in question will appear in **focus,** or "sharp" in the finished film. In between shots, the **set dresser** will use tape to mark the location of key pieces of furniture.

martini: Crew nickname for the very last **shot** of the day on the schedule, the one just before **wrap**, so named because the next shot after that is "out of a glass." Synonyms include the *window shot* and *LFS.*

master shot: Also called **establishing shot**. Normally done with a **wide-angle** lens, a master shot runs for the duration of a particular **scene** and must contain all the key **dialogue** and **story points**, in case there isn't time to film anything else. It's easiest to light the largest areas of the set first, so any good movie **crew** will shoot the master shot first. Next come the **close-ups**, termed "going in for **cov-**

erage." In all subsequent shots, **actors** have to use the same body English, hold the drinks with the correct hand, and smoke cigarettes of the same length, in order to match the master angle. They are aided in this quest by timely suggestions by the **script supervisor**.

matte painting: All the great fantasy mountains, impossible landscapes, and castles in the old Hollywood films are actually photographed paintings rendered on glass by Albert Whitlock (1915–1999). Between 1934 and 1992, he worked on more than 130 movies. They placed the glass, on which part of the **scene** is actually painted, out in front of the camera and then photographed normally. This technique places the **actors** into the painted background, though it limits their freedom of movement somewhat. The effect of these simple matte shots is pretty good, as long as they're left on the screen only a few seconds. Today computers are used for backgrounds and landscapes, and the result is the *Lord of the Rings* series of films.

mattebox: This is the secret movie term for the **sunshade** on the front of the **lens**. It's called the *mattebox* because of the obsolete practice (last attempted in the 1950s) of mounting reference cutouts, gelatin filters, **matte paintings**, and the like in front of the camera during **effects** shots. Computers have made cutout mattes history, but we still use a big mattebox to hold glass **filters** for everyday shooting.

MAW: Insider showbiz slang for "model, actress, . . . whatever!" For some reason, models often want to develop into actresses, even though it may actually entail a pay cut. Famous former-model actresses include Farrah Fawcett, Jaclyn Smith, Geena Davis, and Andie MacDowell. Further training may be required to become a "spokesmodel."

maxi-brute, mini-brute: Though reasonably small, the maxi- and mini-brutes are extremely bright and powerful banks of lights. They are often used by film crews when working at night to light up the side of a building, or to light an entire hillside or city street when suspended from a **snorkel lift**.

meat ax: Motivational tool for renegotiating a higher salary with a recalcitrant **producer**. Also, a really big rectangular **flag**. See **teaser**.

medic: Minor injuries to **cast** and **crew** can slow production schedules, so a medic is available on staff for all Hollywood shoots. They dispense vitamins, Tums, etc., and sometimes they get a chance to really shine (see **stunts**). On **location** in NYC, producers have determined that there are fine hospitals everywhere within walking distance, so *no* medic. Sorry. You can help yourself to a bandage or some chewing gum at the **craft-service** table.

medium shot: Not a **close-up**, but not a **full shot** either, the *medium shot* is a fuzzy term that means a shot including the actor's head and shoulders (like Dan Rather on the news . . . a close shot, but not too close).

method acting: Instead of just pretending to be someone else, or "acting," many of today's leading movie **thespians** rely on the teachings of the old dead Russian stage director Stanislavsky to help them prepare for a role. This generally requires totally inhabiting the world of that person (whether the role is based on a real person or is fictional) in an attempt to more or less *become* them. Actors will often go to great lengths to achieve reality in a performance. If the

STRIKE THE BABY AND KILL THE BLONDE | **129**

movie role calls for a drug-crazed street person . . . well, you don't have to watch very many *E! True Hollywood Stories* to see where that can lead.

mic: (Pronounced *mike.*) Short for *microphone.* The mics used for recording movie **dialogue** are highly specialized and cost thousands of dollars, yet they are attached to the end of the **boom pole** with simple rubber bands or ponytail elastics. Go figure.

mickey: This electric slang term is short for *mickey mole,* a popular type of **movie light**, unchanged in design since the 1930s. See also **redhead**.

Mickey Rooney: The young actor who costarred with Judy Garland in a number of films. Apparently, he was not well liked by film workers, because in movie slang, a slow **dolly** move is referred to on **set** as a Mickey Rooney—a little creep.

mighty: Short for *mighty mole,* the big brother of **mickey**. A type of two-kilowatt movie light made by Mole-Richardson company in **Hollywood**, California. See **blonde**.

mime: To pantomime—that is, to pretend to talk. On a movie, all the **background** players and **extras** mime instead of talking out loud; after all, it is the star's **dialogue** we wish to hear.

mirrors: Used by the **actors** and **makeup** artists, of course, but contrary to the cliché "smoke and mirrors," actual glass mirrors are rarely used for lighting the **set**. They're expensive and fragile. Sometimes the **grips** create a nice "swimming pool" lighting effect by placing broken mirror glass in a pan of water and shining a light into it, but first you have to locate someone on the **crew** who isn't superstitious to break the mirror.

mise-en-scène: Here's a phrase that's handy in conversations with academic film critics, like James Lipton from *Inside the Actors Studio*. (Warning—to avoid ridicule, do not ever use this phrase on a real movie **set**! The **grips** will pound you.) It means all the elements, the atmosphere, and the textures that add up to the whole visual filmic enchilada. The mise-en-scène of *Jaws* is a wonderful watery world populated by predatory sharks and fragile human beings . . . something like that.

Mitchell: Mitchell Corporation's cameras dominated **Hollywood** filmmaking between World War II and 1970. All the classic films you might name from that period were shot with Mitchell cameras. They were rugged, dependable, and quiet. Unfortunately, they were also gigantic (over seventy-five pounds), and Mitchells were completely supplanted by **Panavision** motion-picture cameras in the 1970s. Digital imaging systems are now knocking on Panavision's door. What goes around comes around.

mix: This refers to the **soundtrack**, and the interplay of all the various sound sources, such as **dialogue**, music, **foley** sounds, and so on. Can't hear the lead actor, and the loud music gives away the surprise ending? Time to fix the mix. See **EQ**.

mixer: The sound mixer is the head of the **sound department**, who records the **actor's dialogue** live on the **set** and oversees placement of the **mics**. He or she works at a movable **sound cart** that houses a digital audiotape or analog Nagra tape recorder, **radio mics**, spare **boom poles**, cables, what have you. Worst blunder by newbies on a movie set: putting a full coffee cup on top of the sound cart!

model: In **special effects** filmmaking, a model generally refers to a scaled-down version of, say, the Titanic or Mount Everest, which might be easier for filming than the real thing. Computers haven't completely done away with models. Often a combination of models and **CGI** are used, as in *The Perfect Storm*. Director Wolfgang Petersen used scale model boats splashing around in a **studio** water tank, mixed with huge ocean waves generated by computers, courtesy of **ILM**.

money: The reason the **crew** works twelve to fourteen hours a day on films to begin with. That, and the opportunity to hang out with movie **stars**. On a working **set**, the *money* means the main star, as in "Don't worry about the **extras** in this **shot**, just focus the **camera** on the money!"

monologue: Talking to yourself. Or to the audience. Or to another **actor** who doesn't interrupt, not like in real life. Otherwise that's **dialogue**.

montage: A French word that literally means "editing," and is used to denote a jumble of individual **shots** that, when viewed together, describe a single **theme**. Sylvester Stallone as Rocky Balboa preparing for the big fight and a couple falling in love at the beach are two good examples. A montage can be shorthand for the passage of time and stand in for several **scenes'** worth of regular character development. **Cut to the chase**.

MOS: A very common phrase, heard every day on the film **set** and nowhere else. *MOS* means filming with camera only, with no sound recording. A German director in Hollywood once said, "Now ve vill film mit out sound!" and the shorthand stuck. Strange but 100 percent true.

motion control: *Motion control* refers to a **camera** system controlled by a computer. The computer isn't generating the images, but rather it's controlling the movements of an otherwise standard movie camera. This is used quite a bit in **special effects, animation**, and **model** photography.

motion-picture film: Invented by Edison and George Eastman over a hundred years ago, currently made only by Kodak and Fuji. It's 35 mm film very similar to the film you might put in your Nikon, except that it comes in gigantic four-hundred- and one-thousand-foot rolls and is sent through the camera vertically. The film can be balanced for daylight or artificial lighting.

motivation: This is actor-speak for the underlying psychological driving force behind their character's action. "Hey, Spielberg, what's my motivation?" A large paycheck.

Moviecam: One of the big three companies that manufacture high-quality motion picture cameras. (The others are **Arri** and **Panavision**.) Moviecams are designed and built in Austria and are lightweight, robust, and quiet. And expensive—over a hundred thousand bucks. See **rental house**.

movie light: They come in all sizes, from 100-watt **inkys** to 18,000-watt **HMIs**, and the movie company generally travels with one or more huge tractor-trailer trucks filled from floor to ceiling with lights. Specialized lighting units to highlight the movie **stars** is one reason that **Hollywood** movies look a little better than home videos. Talented **hair and makeup** artists working overtime is another.

moving on: When a **shot** is completed to the **director's** satisfaction, the **AD** motivates the **crew** by shouting, "We've got that shot . . . moving on!" This has the right blend of finality and encouragement. One phrase isn't enough for this transition, and synonyms you might hear include "New deal!" "FDR!" and **"turning around."**

MOW: Movie of the week—you know, a movie shot specifically for TV, like *Return to Gilligan's Island* or *Baby Jessica—Stuck Headfirst in a Well!* Rarely filmed in L.A. these days (see **runaway production**), MOWs are filmed mostly in Canada to save money. You can enjoy listening for Canadian phrases like "aboot the hoose" and "Eh?" while you watch . . . and keep a sharp lookout for those clean Toronto streets, supposedly doubling for NYC! I've photographed several films in Toronto *(Short Circuit II, Sea of Love, Family Pictures)*, and one trick is to have the **prop** department carry piles of trash that can be added to street **shots** for extra realism.

music videos: These are, in the immortal words of Frank Zappa, "shitty little movies." I'm not sure if that's fair, but it makes for a pithy quote. Rock or rap music videos with any kind of budget are usually shot with *film* **cameras**, despite the name. MTV has influenced many aspects of modern life, not the least of which is the way **Hollywood features** and **commercials** are shot today. More images, faster editing, louder **soundtracks**. Video clips can be a lot of fun to work on—just make sure you like the band, as you'll be hearing the same song repeated about one hundred times during the sixteen-hour-long **workday.**

multicamera: Refers to the technique (first used by Abbott and Costello) whereby several **cameras** film the **action** simultaneously.

Often it's more efficient to stage an important **scene** just once and hire a big **crew** and extra cameras to film it. TV shows all use multi-camera techniques when filming sitcoms. **Features** often employ multiple cameras to capture **stunts** and other unrepeatable events. I've done three films with Al Pacino *(Sea of Love, Scent of a Woman, City Hall)*, and we've always used at least two cameras. You just never know when Al will dig deep and deliver an unrepeatable great performance. Aim three cameras at him, and you can't miss.

multiplex: See **cineplex**.

Nagra: High-quality Swiss quarter-inch tape recorders made by Kudelski were the standard for recording on-**set** movie **dialogue** from roughly 1960 to 2000, until DAT, DV, DVD, and all those other digital abbreviations took over.

narrative: (1) A storytelling or scripted film is termed a *narrative film,* as opposed to a **documentary,** a **commercial,** or an **industrial** film. One challenge when creating the new "reality" TV **shows** is the lack of traditional narrative structure. Another challenge is finding enough good-looking babes and dudes who are willing to humiliate themselves for a brief shot at fame.

(2) *Narrative* can be a synonym for **plot.** It refers to the story of a particular film; for example, the narrative of *The Godfather* traces the lives of the Corleone family, exploring this typical Italian family's adjustment to life in a new country.

ND: (1) Nondescript. **ADs** use this term to describe people and things, such as cars, that won't draw undue attention to themselves. "Gimme two ND **background** standing on the corner, now!"

(2) Neutral density. A glass **filter** that transmits light evenly across the visible light spectrum. In other words, gray. It's a gray filter. It's used in front of the **lens** to reduce exposure without affecting **color,** or alternatively you can tape large sheets of ND to windows to reduce streaming sunlight.

negative: (1) Film that has passed through the movie **camera** becomes a negative image, with all the light objects rendered dark, and vice versa. To properly view the **scene**, a positive **print** is made in the **lab**, or a digital copy is made during **film-to-tape** transfer.

(2) *Negative* can also be a synonym for **raw stock**, as in, "How much negative is left in the **darkroom**?"

next big one: As a highly competitive and slightly paranoid **freelance**-based workforce, film workers refer to any possible next assignment in near-mythical terms. "Thanks for a great **shoot**, buddy—see you on the next big one."

NG: No good. Bad. I made a mistake. Oops!

night call, night shoot: Movies often require the **cast** and **crew** to work from 6 p.m. to 6 a.m., instead of the other way around. **Day-for-night** shooting unfortunately is rare these days. To realistically film a dark night **scene** for today's movies, it has to be photographed . . . on a dark night.

nitrate: The old, bad, unstable, and really dangerous film base material, the kind that spontaneously combusts. See **acetate**.

no print: At the end of the day, all the film goes to the **lab**, and the **director** chooses which **takes** are printed and incorporated into the final film. The other not-so-good **shots**—and there are many—are marked NO PRINT. These may someday find a way onto the screen, however. See **director's cut**.

noise reduction: This refers to various electronic techniques by which an original sound signal is preserved, and the offending pops, scratches, and hums are reduced. Two popular noise-reduction systems for movie theaters are **Dolby** Digital and THX (which is owned by movie **director** and wealth-accumulator George Lucas).

normal lens: In between **wide angle** and **telephoto** is the normal lens, though this means different things to different folks. Directors with a background in **commercials**, such as Tony Scott, favor slightly longer lenses, so a normal lens on *Crimson Tide* or *Spy Game* would be 75 to 100 mm, whereas on the Orson Welles classic *Citizen Kane,* 35 mm was more the norm. A normal lens is considered to approximate the view of the human eye.

NTSC: The American video standard. See **PAL** for witticisms and an explanation. If you buy any questionable bootleg videos or DVDs, just make sure it says NTSC on the box, not PAL or SECAM, and it should play in the USA.

NYPD Blue: Hit TV show that has become slang for a particular photography style: Use very little lighting gear, put **telephoto lenses** on the **cameras,** and **pan** the cameras around, featuring shaky **close-ups** on guns, coffee cups, and other props. This approach can inject some visual excitement into an average **screenplay. Directors** on other **shows** understand when I say, "What if I simply *NYPD Blue* on this **take**?" I've occasionally worked on *NYPD Blue* over the past ten years, and the **crew** has developed a unique vocabulary. *Vector, richter,* and *shake and bake* are all top-secret stylistic terms that have special meaning only to workers on *NYPD Blue.* I'm sworn to secrecy.

obie: A light placed atop the camera to illuminate the **actor's** face. (It creates a lovely white highlight reflected in the eyes.) Named for the actress Merle Oberon, who apparently requested an obie and her favorite **DP** Lucien Ballard for every **shot**. Hey, having a light named after you is better than what happened to **Mickey Rooney**.

office: Though films are photographed on **sets** and **practical locations,** they're organized from the office. The **producer** takes a six-month lease and sets up shop; minimum is two phone lines and three or four desks. The office is where prospective **crew** and **cast** members are interviewed, **preproduction** meetings get held, and packages are delivered. During shooting, a skeleton **production** staff mans the office, while the shooting crew is on set, creating movie magic.

offline: Postproduction and **editing** work performed without affecting the ultimate version of a film, such as scoring music, watching screenings, and editing scenes temporarily, are said to be performed offline.

offscreen: Refers to any **action**, sounds, or overheard **dialogue** that may be included generally in the film but doesn't happen within view of the camera. For example, as Roy Scheider battles the shark in *Jaws,* Richard Dreyfuss is underwater, offscreen, peeing in his wetsuit. After the conclusion (the shark explodes after Scheider shoots a bullet into the air tank wedged in the shark's mouth—right!), Dreyfuss reappears at the water's surface . . . **onscreen**.

on hold: Producers often want to line up **cast** and **crew** far in advance of filming, yet aren't willing to pay any sort of guaranteed money. They will instead "put you on hold." This happens a lot on **commercials**. If another offer comes in, you are expected to call the **producer** who has you "on hold," and give them the option of "booking" you (that is, coughing up some money). Some people go so far as to have second- and third-level holds lined up weeks in advance, but I have trouble keeping it all straight. I just start working on one project at a time until either (1) it's completed or (2) I get **fired**. Easy.

on the day: Originating from our friends north of the border, this phrase means "when we actually shoot." On a Toronto film set, you might hear, "Aboot the trucks . . . on the day, we'll have to move the **honeywagon**, it's in the **shot**!"

one-er: This is an entire **scene** done in one long continuous **shot**, with no **close-ups**. *All the President's Men, The Player,* and *Goodfellas* all have terrific one-ers. I shot a very nice single-take scene for M. Night Shyamalan's *Wide Awake,* which featured a young boy and his grandpa (Robert Loggia) debating the existence of God. Today's moviegoers, raised on MTV and video games, seem to prefer stories told in many jumbled rapid-fire shots. See *The Fast and the Furious.* That pretty much describes the filming style, as well. No one-ers.

one-liner: This is a **shooting schedule** condensed to one descriptive sentence per scene, designed for those with limited time and attention spans, such as **grips, gaffers,** and **camera operators**. Toward the end of **principal photography** when finances are tight, the easiest way for the film to save money is for the **producer** to tear off and discard the last three or four pages of the one-liner schedule.

online: Online editing is the expensive process during which all the factors such as music, sound, visual effects, and picture are brought together by the **editor** into a harmonious whole. Hopefully. *Online* refers specifically to the final real-time arranging of all these elements.

onscreen: Anything that's captured by the **camera** ends up onscreen. Some **story points** are merely alluded to, or are simply not shown in the film and are therefore considered to have happened **offscreen**.

open call: A casting session for an upcoming film or play that is open to everyone. Many are called . . . few are chosen. See **cattle call**.

open mic: A microphone signal being successfully sent to the **sound department**. Make a note: With today's wireless technology, if you're ever asked to star in a movie, make sure to take your **mic** *completely off* whenever leaving the **set** and engaging in impromptu sexual escapades. There is a chance the sounds will be broadcast via an open mic for the benefit of everyone within listening range. It's been known to happen.

operator: Synonymous with **camera operator**. Yours truly.

optical: Until digital editing systems from **Avid** and **Final Cut Pro** took over the industry, all fades, **dissolves**, and many **FX** shots required an extra printing step by the **lab,** termed an *optical.* Opticals were generally expensive, and the extra printing step required contributed to a slightly lower image quality.

option: Once a novel hits the best-seller list, the phone calls from Hollywood **producers** aren't far behind. They will pay to "option" the book, to buy the rights to *try* to make a movie out of the book, for a set period of time, say one to three years. The book author gets a fee (anything from one to fifty thousand dollars) for doing essentially nothing, as they've already completed the book. Other **screenwriters** are hired to hammer out the **screenplay.** If the movie project ever gets off the ground, a larger fee is then paid to the book author. If the project goes nowhere (usually the case), the author doesn't have to return the option money; in fact, he or she might sell another option on the same book to another producer.

Oscar: Academy Award. Still waiting for the phone call . . .

outtakes: You know what these bloopers are: **shots** that don't make it into the finished film, usually **actors** flubbing the **dialogue.** The first film to include outtakes during the end **credits** was Hal Ashby's *Being There,* starring Peter Sellers. Thanks to comedic performers like Eddie Murphy and Jim Carrey, the outtakes are sometimes better than the film you just paid nine bucks to see.

overcrank: Film cameras normally run at a speed of twenty-four individual frames recorded each second. If you film a **shot** with a camera running at forty-eight fps, the resulting projected film will be apparently slowed down by 50 percent, and the images will appear in slow motion. Overcranked film looks much more detailed than its video slo-mo counterpart. Compare the timeless look of classic NFL films from 1960 to 1990 (most of which were shot with small 16 mm film cameras, slightly overcranked) to live video footage from the same era.

overhead: On the movie **set,** an overhead is a large (twelve-by-twelve feet or larger) net or white parachute silk supported by **hi boys,** used to soften the effects of direct sunlight.

overlap: When the **actors** can't wait to say their **lines,** and in fact interrupt their fellow **thespians,** it is called "stepping on the lines" or overlapping. This can be a good thing, and make the **dialogue** seem natural, especially in a **master shot.** However, it does make editing between **close-ups** difficult, so when filming **singles,** the **director** usually instructs the actors to pause slightly before speaking, to "watch the overlaps."

over-the-shoulder (OTS): A type of **shot** first tried by the great **DP** Gregg Toland in the 1930s while working with Orson Welles. The **camera** is lined up behind one actor's shoulder (who appears in half the frame) and a **medium shot** of the other actor, facing the camera, is filmed. This type of shot shows the actor and the person he's addressing in the same shot. Though revolutionary at the time, the OTS has become standard on all films and TV shows.

PA: No one says *gofer*. That's a **Hollywood** cliché, the same as "**Take five!**" and **klieg light**. The entry-level movie job is production assistant. Many of today's top industry professionals (including yours truly) started at the bottom as lowly PAs. Every film carries five to ten PAs, who work long hours and are whipped into shape by the key PA and the **AD**. Pay is $50 to $125 a day. Keep track of your workdays for about three years—maybe you'll get into the **DGA**. Maybe.

page: This is the network television (not film set) equivalent of **PA**. The craft **unions** won't allow untrained people to handle **props**, lights, or **cameras**, so pages end up as sort of glorified interns– secretaries–tour guides.

page count: To film a hundred-page movie script on a thirty-three-day schedule, you have to film three pages per day. Pages are broken down into eighths, and all schedules reflect the anticipated page count for each day. A $7^2/_8$-page **scene** might all take place sitting around a table, and possibly be filmed by the crew in one afternoon. Then again, "The cavalry charges—the Indians fight back" takes only an eighth of a page to *write* but three weeks to *film*. **Producers** keep close tabs on the page count! Once you shoot all the pages, they can stop spending money and **pull the plug**.

PAL: Specifically, this stands for *phase alternating line,* but what it really means is that you can't play a European DVD or video on a TV in the United States. The technical standards are different. Ever travel abroad to discover your hair dryer power plug won't fit into their socket? Same deal with video signals. France adopted yet a third standard, as did Africa, called SECAM. Japan is on our team, however, adopting our NTSC standard. I hear they are also big fans of our national pastime, baseball.

pan: The act of swiveling the **camera** about, thus moving the picture horizontally. A panning **shot** sees more of the **action** than a static **frame**. In the heat of battle, even experienced film people get *pan* and its opposite term **tilt** mixed up. Pan up! Tilt left! Come on!

pan and scan: After a polite warning from the FBI, a film on VHS or DVD might explain, "This film has been reformatted to fit onto your television." The original **wide-screen** cinema version has had the sides chopped off the picture to match the **aspect ratio** of your TV set. Essential **action** needs to be included, so a technician views each **shot** and reframes (pans and scans) accordingly. See also **letterbox**. These days, improvements in software allow for relatively smooth optical **pans**, but films that underwent pan and scan during a **film-to-tape** transfer anytime before the new millennium will probably exhibit some annoying jitters.

pancake: A small square of plywood that can be used on **set** to level furniture and **actors**. See **man-maker**.

Panatape, PanaHead, Pana (whatever): Like McDonald's, **Panavision** finds it necessary to stick its name on every piece of gear the company makes. If you want to distinguish members of the **camera**

crew from other casually dressed film workers on a **set**, look for the ones wearing freebie PANAVISION T-shirts.

Panavision: (1) The very best studio 35 mm movie **cameras** in the world are virtually handmade in Woodland Hills, California, USA. The flexibility, reliability, and ergonomic design of the Panavision system make them a favorite with camera **crews** and **producers** alike.

(2) *Panavision* can be synonymous with **anamorphic**, a **wide-screen** photographic process utilizing special **lenses**.

panorama: The whole wide view in front of you from side to side. Also used to describe a big, big, really big wide **shot**, like the shot from the top of Tom Hanks's island in *Castaway*.

Panther: This is an overengineered German-built **Elemack**-style **camera dolly** that comes in about twenty complicated individual pieces, which the **grips** are meant to quickly reconfigure for each **shot**. Many formerly easy-to-perform manual functions are electronic and computer-controlled on the Panther. Unfortunately, **actors** aren't robots, and they tend to be a little unpredictable. Better to have a human being at the controls of the dolly, even if it is a **grip**.

paparazzi: Annoying freelance photographers unaffiliated with the movie **company** sometimes hang around the **set** trying to snap photos of the **stars** to sell to local papers. The name itself derives from "Paparazzo," a film character in Fellini's *La Dolce Vita*. Occasionally, paparazzi can provide some entertainment for the working **crew,** as they skulk around, and will generally go to great lengths to get a picture. I remember one dedicated individual climbed into a trash Dumpster in order to sneak a shot of Helen Hunt during the filming of an episode of *Mad About You*. Good job!

PAR: Gaffers and lighting designers are always trying to cheat the laws of physics and electricity in an attempt to maximize lamp output. A PAR is a powerful lamp that gets its strong beam from a *para*bolic reflector in the back of the metal lamp housing. The curved surface collects and intensifies the resulting light beam.

parallel: Scaffolding erected in sections by the **grips** to support **cameras,** lights, and people is called a parallel. For safety, it needs to be perfectly level and straight, with all crosspieces perfectly parallel, especially when building one several stories high.

parking PA: Okay, this may stretch your imagination a little, so stay with me. While the movie **crew** is shooting on a NYC street, a group of **PAs** goes to the next day's **location,** puts up NO PARKING signs, places orange cones in all available parking places, and then physically guards these spots. They sleep in their cars at night, ready to spring awake to defend their turf against crafty NYC would-be parkers. When the shooting crew arrives with the equipment trucks the next day at sunrise, the parking PAs will grab a **breakfast burrito** and start the process all over again. The glamorous movie life!

pat 'em down: The **actors** can become shiny with perspiration from the hot movie lights, and before a take, the **DP** or **AD** might ask the makeup artist to use a powder puff to dry an actor's face. Actually, sometime around 1996, the "dry look" became passé, and now for extra realism, "sweat" is often added to the actors with bottled French Evian water. See **spritz**.

payroll company: Producers usually contract with a professional accounting firm to be "employers of record" for a film, and to issue weekly paychecks to the **cast** and **crew**.

pelican: Jury-rigged clamp made from modified Vise-Grip pliers that is used by **grips** to hold unwieldy big pieces of **foam core**. Named because of its resemblance to a pelican's beak. Actually, it looks more like a pelican that's been run over by a steamroller.

per diem: Latin term meaning "daily." Movie **crews** working out of town in addition to their salaries are paid a daily stipend of twenty-five to fifty dollars for meals, laundry, gambling, whatever.

period piece: A film set in the past is very rewarding and sometimes difficult for members of the **props, costumes,** and **art departments**. These period pieces might require anything from dozens of 1970s automobiles to hoop skirts. The **Academy** has always looked favorably upon period dramas come **Oscar** time. *Chicago, Shakespeare in Love,* and *The English Patient* are a few examples.

perms: Nothing to do with curly hair. As in "up in the perms"— the permanent high walkways suspended from the interior ceiling of giant **Hollywood** studio **soundstages**, from which lights and **flags** can be hung. Wear a safety harness.

persistence of vision: This is the scientific explanation for what happens between your eyes and brain while viewing movies. The human retina retains for a split second an image of whatever it has just seen. A movie is a sequence of twenty-four individual still pictures projected each second, but the **flicker** should be unnoticeable. Your eye–brain combination integrates the **frames** into a continuous action. Children's flip books work in the same way.

Phil Collins: Sometimes the **DP** will call for a two-foot-square piece of **bounce board** to fill the **actor's** eyes with soft light for a **close-up.** Hip independent **crew** people in NYC refer to this as a *Phil Collins*—small, white, and square.

photo double: When an **extra** physically resembles a particular movie **star**, he or she may be picked as a photo double. As long as the **DP** doesn't **zoom** the camera in too closely, the double can be used for **master shots,** driving shots, and the like. Photo doubles, **body doubles, stand-ins,** and **stunt doubles** are different variations of the same theme—people who work on a film because of a physical resemblance to someone famous. For example, Adam Bryant has been standing in for Robin Williams for years. I first met him on the set of *Jumanji* and then again recently on *House of D* nearly ten years later. Nice work if you can get it.

pick it up: For a **studio** to assume the expenses of distributing a completed **independent** movie to theaters is to pick it up. Also, when a network or other TV outlet agrees to buy a certain number of episodes of a series, they pick it up.

pickup shot: Nearly the same as an **insert shot**, yet slightly different. If a just-completed shot is *almost* perfect, the **director** may choose to reshoot only the flawed section; this is called "shooting a pickup." They trust in the magic of **editing** to join the two shots seamlessly.

picture car: The car being photographed for the movie, often driven by the lead **actors**. Different cars might be filmed at various times (see **insert trailer**), but the picture car is the **hero**.

picture's up: The **AD** calls this phrase out to **cast** and **crew** on **set** just prior to filming, which indicates **rehearsal** is over and the next **shot** will be committed to film. **"Roll sound!"**

pigeon: This piece of **grip** gear looks nothing like its namesake. It's actually a $5/8 \times 3$-inch metal stud mounted to a board and used for holding small lighting instruments. Some U.S. crews call it a "beaverboard." On the film *Virus*, my boss decided this was nasty and sexist, and he instructed everyone to refer to it as a "penis plate" instead. Much better.

pilot: TV **shows** are costly to produce (understatement), and the first trial episode of any potential series is termed a *pilot*. **Producers** and **directors** of this single pilot episode often receive a percentage of a hit show's profits for *years*. **Actors** will often agree to appear in pilots for reasonable rates in exchange for the possibility that the pilot might be **picked up**. Later on, when the show is a big hit like *Friends* or *The Sopranos*, the **actors** occasionally try to renegotiate higher salaries by threatening to leave.

pitch: To toss your **screenplay** idea for the next **Hollywood** blockbuster film to a **producer**. The classic pitch is to describe your potential film idea in relation to other well-known hits. "*Waterworld*—it's just like *Mad Max* and *Road Warrior* . . . in the middle of the ocean!"

plant mic: This is used more by the FBI than sound **mixers** on movies. The highest-quality movie **soundtrack** is usually recorded by waving around a **mic** on a **boom pole**, something to which the **actors**

are all accustomed. Occasionally, for various reasons, the **sound department** will resort to other techniques, such as a tiny microphone hidden inside a lamp, in a car, or behind a saltshaker on a table. The wires must be snaked around and hidden from **camera** view, as well.

plate: Slang for the projected background image when shooting **rear** or **front projection**, or the painted element in a **matte painting**. The background plate is one element of the final composite image and is normally photographed first.

plot: A condensed description of what happens in the film. An example: "Each of us longs for that which we cannot possess" is the **theme** of *The Maltese Falcon,* whereas the plot might be described as "Joel Cairo, Sam Spade, and an all-star cast chase around shooting at each other in an attempt to obtain a worthless statue of an ugly bird." The plot is a description of the **action**, such as you might find on the VHS box or in an airline magazine.

POC: Production Office Coordinator. They work directly under the **line producer** and unit production manager (**UPM**), and make sure all the film gear and people are in the right place at the right time. They cover the production office while the crew is on **location**. Strong verbal skills and a pleasant telephone manner are a must.

Polaroid: Instant **cameras** are used to aid the **continuity, props,** and **vanities** in matching all the various shots. Need to determine where a particular chair goes or which side of the **actor's** face needs a fake scar for scene 11A? Check the Polaroid picture. These are slowly being replaced by digital pictures and laptops.

poor man's process: For every expensive, time-consuming movie technique, there is also a corresponding cheaper way. Poor man's process is when you photograph people in cars and they *pretend* to be moving, when in fact they're sitting completely still. Used on both low-budget TV **shows** *(The A-Team)* and expensive movies *(Bugsy)*. Our insert trailer broke an axle while filming *I'm Not Rappaport* one night in NYC. Time was tight. We simply left the car parked where it was in the middle of the West Side Highway, the **grips** jiggled the car's chassis with long two-by-four boards . . . voilà! Walter Matthau and Ossie Davis look exactly like they're riding down the road!

pop-up: If a heavy rain falls, the movie **crew** frantically erects temporary eight-by-eight tents, such as the ones manufactured by EZ UP, in order to protect the expensive movie equipment. Curiously, the movie **camera** is usually covered with a simple garbage bag. Whatever works.

positive: A photographic image where white is rendered as white, blue is blue, and so on. The movie **print** that runs through the projector at the **cineplex** is a positive image, whereas the film that emerges from the **camera** after shooting is an unprocessed **negative**.

postproduction: The third phase of movie production (following **preproduction** and **principal photography**), also called *post*. Post is where the **editor** works his or her magic, the images are manipulated digitally, music is added, and the **dialogue** might be rerecorded. See **ADR**. Postproduction on a **Hollywood** film usually takes anywhere from one to four months.

postproduction house: A facility dedicated to finishing films that have progressed beyond **principal photography**. These can provide a myriad of services, including editing, sound recording, **film-to-tape** transfers, and **special effects**.

POV: Here's an example of a groovy film school word that one actually hears pretty often on the **set**. When the **camera** is placed exactly where a character in the scene was previously standing, the resulting **shot** is termed that character's point of view (POV). The opposite is an objective angle, when the camera is placed to the side or overhead. Some **directors** become obsessed with making nearly every shot someone's POV. When I worked on *Jumanji*, we had a lengthy discussion regarding the proper way to achieve a charging rhinoceros's POV shot.

practical: On a movie **set**, this is any everyday item that actually works, such as a lamp that lights up, a phone that rings, or a sink with a drain. The **art department** usually places practical lights around the set, hooks up telephones, and tends to the plumbing. If nature calls, just make sure the toilet you're using on the corner of the **set** is a real one, not a **prop**.

practical effects: These are all the rubber-band and fishing-line tricks used by the **prop department** during filming. Gently falling snow, torrential rain, and atmospheric **smoke** likewise fall under the heading of *practical effects*. Computers have taken over many aspects of filmmaking these days, but good cheap practical effects will always have their place.

practical location: A place that's not always a movie **set**, such as a working business, someone's apartment—you get the idea. Sometimes these are not very "practical" in terms of convenience for **feature**-film photography. Real bathrooms (unless you live in a Trump-size mansion) are way too small to hold the necessary **lights**, **camera**, **actors**, and **crew**. For this reason, movie bathrooms are nearly always built as a set with removable walls on a **film stage**.

premiere: This is the first time the finished film is seen by the public, though the crowd is usually stacked with press (see **press party**) and **studio** lackeys. The **stars** get dolled up, arrive in front of the **house** to great fanfare, and walk the red carpet. **Klieg lights** sweep the city skyline. The real moviemakers (**producer, director**, and **editor**) usually hide in back of the theater, having already seen the  film dozens of times. They nervously await the crowd's response. An enthusiastic premiere crowd is the equivalent of the live theater standing ovation, validation for months of hard work.

prep: When the **DP, AD, director**, and **producer** are in **preproduction** on a film and are scouting **locations**, hiring **crew**, and traveling a lot, they're said to be prepping. *In prep* can also be an all-purpose cover for a struggling **producer** or **director** in highly competitive **Hollywood**. In this context, "He's in prep on a film" might be code for "He's in substance-abuse rehab following a nervous breakdown."

press kit: This is a bag of goodies (T-shirts, hats) and promo stuff (videotapes, bios, flyers) given to members of the press during a film's initial marketing campaign, timed to coincide with the film's release.

press party: Boozy bacchanals thrown by the **studios** for members of the fourth estate, dedicated to lubricating the machinery of public opinion in the hopes of receiving positive reviews.

preview: Sophisticated film people call *coming attractions* at the multiplex *trailers,* whereas *previews* are audience test screenings for

COMING ATTRACTIONS

films during the later stages of completion. **Studios** spend a lot of time, money, and energy previewing their **product** for audiences of carefully selected average moviegoers. Of course, these are all sixteen-year-old mall rats who happen to reside in the San Fernando Valley. The audiences vote and approve everything from the star's hairdo and sex appeal to the movie's ending. Adrian Lyne's film *Fatal Attraction* is one famous case where a film's ending was completely reshot following an unenthusiastic preview screening. Hey, if you want Glenn Close's character to die—you got it! She's toast!

prime lens: **Zoom lenses** can bring you closer to the **action** with a turn of a knob, but prime lenses are designed and built with a single fixed **focal length** (50 mm, 100 mm, and so forth). Top **feature** film **cinematographers** often use primes and switch between lenses for each **shot,** as they deliver slightly sharper pictures than zooms.

Primo: Italian word meaning "preeminent." Primo is a trademark of **Panavision** and refers to their outstanding series of **lenses,** made for them by Leitz in Canada. Okay, some good things besides back bacon, TV movies, and Molson come from the frozen northland after all. Primos offer fantastic clarity, color rendition, and user-friendliness. They're simply the best.

principal actor: Someone with a featured speaking role, not an **extra.** They generally have their names on the **call sheet** and on the backs of **director's chairs.** If they're big **stars,** they might also get **main title credits.**

principal photography: The middle third of the moviemaking process, coming in between **preproduction** and **postproduction**. During principal photography, the **actors** act, the cameras are **rolled**, and the images are indelibly recorded for posterity. Well, they were fairly indelible before computers.

print: The film that goes through the **camera on set** is later soaked in chemicals by the lab and becomes a **negative** image. You need to shine some light through it again and make a **positive print** for proper viewing and projection. Often the printing stage is skipped altogether until editing is complete. The modern practice is for the **director** and other **grown-ups** to view videotape **dailies** made during a **film-to-tape** transfer each day directly from the negative.

print it: When the **director** is captivated by the images on the **video assist** monitor, he does a quick check with the **DP** and then shouts, "Print it!" The **script supervisor** circles the take number in his or her logbook, and the director then has the choice of whether to **move on** or **go again**.

process: Synonymous with **rear projection**. A good example of process is the classic driving shot, with the movie star behind the wheel in the studio, and the background supplied by a different **crew**, photographed on a different day. The believability of the effect can be helped by perfectly matching the lighting of the **foreground** with the **background plate**. It's also important for the **talent** to turn the steering wheel in the appropriate direction.

producer: In many ways, this is really the person making the movie, if you take into account all the financial, artistic, and personnel decisions. The producer hires the **director**, supervises the rewriting of the **script**, **pitches** the story idea to the **studio**, oversees **casting**, and begs for money from the **executive producer**. Once the movie actually starts **principal photography**, however, the director is in the driver's seat, and the producer's work is pretty much done. Time to take some meetings for the **next big one**.

product placement: See that Coke can, that Sony TV, that corporate logo stretched across Bruce Willis's T-shirt? Chances are the movie's **producer** has already telephoned the advertising people and received a big fee. Sometime around 1988, producers realized that it would look more realistic to use familiar products as movie **props,** and extort—I mean request—some money for these advertisements . . . cleverly hidden within the film. Get ready for a lot more sneaky commercial messages on TV, as advertisers and producers try to outsmart audiences who have grown accustomed to TV remotes, TiVos, and fast-forward buttons.

product shot: On a **commercial**, once the **crew**'s energy is totally spent at the very end of a sixteen-hour **workday**, it's time to photograph the product shot! This is a picture of the **client's** product, with the slogan superimposed on the TV screen. There is an art to shooting a great product shot—hey, nothing is more important than making the client's stuff look good. Actors are often sent home for the day (no overtime pay for you!), and product shots are normally filmed last on the schedule.

production: When you telephone the **office** of any film in progress, the person answering the line invariably says, "Production!" When used this way, the word describes the movie **company**, with an emphasis on the present. The production is the group of **freelance** people assembled to realize the film, and also the shooting of the film itself, synonymous with **principal photography**.

production assistant: See **PA.** Lowly yet indispensable **crew** member, entry-level position.

production designer: Person responsible for the overall "look" of the film. They **scout locations** with the **director,** design original **sets** with the **art director,** and consult (argue) with the **DP** about elements of style. Moviemaking is a collaborative art form, and one of the film director's main sounding boards throughout the film is the production designer.

production manager: See **UPM.**

production report: The document of everything that happens daily on **set,** maintained and creatively written by the **assistant directors** for the benefit of absentee **producers,** accountants, and lawyers. In a perfect world, it would read like the day's **call sheet,** everything executed perfectly to plan. In reality, it is more a document of everything that goes wrong. **Honeywagon** got a flat tire? Movie **star** hungover and late for work? A pickup truck ran over the **director's** toy poodle? It's all in the production report, baby.

production supervisor: (1) This is a person working under the **UPM** and directly above the **POC,** yet there is no catchy abbreviation for this job title. The production supervisor is an essential **crew** member, ultimately responsible for juggling all the people, places, and things necessary for filming.

(2) Sometimes the money people in L.A. will send a high-level **producer** to oversee (babysit) the film when things are going wrong,

and just before calling the **bond company**. The **studio** term for this position is likewise *production supervisor*.

projection: The art of shining light through a celluloid filmstrip, thereby casting the resulting image onto a screen. Add some speakers, sticky seats, and popcorn—you've got a movie theater. At least, that's the way it's done now. On the horizon is all-digital projection. This will allow for **prints** of current films to be transmitted to theaters and stored electronically. The switchover will happen as soon as the **studios** determine ways to maximize profits and guard against Internet piracy.

projectionist: This used to be the cranky old **union** guy changing huge reels of film in the back of a large, well-decorated, beautiful movie house. Now it's the cranky college kid changing huge reels of film in the back of the tiny multiplex. Soon it will be the cranky teenager downloading *Star Wars: Episode 17—The Return of Jar Jar Binks,* directly from Sony's orbiting satellite.

prompter: In the live theater, a little man hides in front of the stage to help the actors remember their lines ("To be or . . ."). On a movie **set**, it falls to the **script supervisor** to shout out the missing words for the perplexed **thespian**. This happens a lot during rehearsals, but if the **actor** blows a line during filming, we'll just edit out that bit and film it again. And again. And again . . .

prop department: Two to five individuals whose job it is to assemble and prepare all the **props**, things held by **actors** during the filming. In a pinch, they'll help rearrange furniture on the **set**, but that's really the job of the **dresser**.

prop master: Top of the props, the person in charge of all the lamps, chairs, food eaten by actors, guns, and so forth.

props: Properties. These are things placed specifically around the **set**, or carried by the **actors**. The props department has a big truck filled with food, telephones, cigarettes, pistols, silverware . . . basically everything you would need for a good after-hours party. They're constantly loading or unloading the truck and scurrying to or from the set in an attempt to supply the perfect prop for the **scene** being filmed. If you need any kind of help on **set**, just yell, "Props!" and watch 'em run!

proscenium: The curved archway at the front of a theater building that separates the seats from the stage. *Proscenium* is also a useful buzz phrase **directors** like to sling about, which refers to the physical and psychological separation between the **camera** and the **actors**. For example, the fourth wall is always missing on **sitcoms**; the cameras remain *in front* of the imagined proscenium, which contributes to the "stagy" feel. Movies shooting with **single-camera** techniques can break with this convention, using a variety of techniques. See **cinema verité, handheld, Steadicam.**

proxar: See **diopter**. These special **filters** allow focusing the movie **camera** on very close objects, such as letters and computer screens.

PSA: Public service announcement. The big TV networks will broadcast for free **commercials** made by nonprofit companies that are, in their judgment, valuable to everybody, such as how to fight forest fires or crime or AIDs. Workers filming PSAs generally agree to defer their salaries in exchange for a personal tax write-off. All for a good cause . . .

publicist: For the best explanation of what a publicist does, see Billy Crystal's great performance in *America's Sweethearts*. During the filming, they arrange the photographer and reporter access to the **director** and **stars**. Once the film is **in the can,** they manage the press and promotion for a film.

pull-back: On a TV **show,** this is the suggestion offered by the **director,** meaning to **zoom** wider, showing more of the **set**. On a

feature film being shot with **prime lenses,** this means to move the **dolly** backward, away from the **actor.** A well-executed and stylish pull-back reveals new information to the viewer, such as a **foreground** gun, or a **baddie** unseen by our **hero** lurking at the **edge of frame.**

pull focus: The art of estimating the distance between the **movie star** and the front of the **camera,** and the simultaneous turning of the **lens** to the appropriate marking, performed by the 1st **AC** during a shot. Simply put, the **focus puller** adjusts the lens, and the **camera operator** points the camera. That's it, the secret of movie photography right there. Hire a good assistant, and point the camera in the right direction.

pull the plug: This is when the **workday** has become overextended and the **producer** steps in to halt the filming. **Directors** rarely like it when producers pull rank on them in this manner, but there's only twenty-four hours in a day. They like it even less when the **studio** steps in to permanently cancel their project, preferring to take a loss rather than risk a potential box office **turkey.** This is also referred to as *pulling the plug.*

punch-out week: Veterans of any intense competitive **freelance** project will instantly recognize the meaning of the term. On any long movie shoot, one to two weeks before the project finishes, tempers flare and things come to a head. Words are exchanged, summary firings often result, and actual fisticuffs are not unknown. During the last week of the project, everyone becomes best friends again. "See you on the **next big one**, buddy!"

push-in: You got it, the opposite of **pull-back**. A push-in entails **zooming** in or dollying forward. A little movement can be used to subtly heighten a dramatic moment. Alternatively, you can quickly shove the **dolly** around to inject some excitement into a **commercial** or rock **video**.

push one: Film that has been underexposed (either by shooting without lights, shooting at night, or both) can be helped in the **lab** by leaving it in the developing soup of chemicals for an extended period of time. An increase in **exposure** of 100 percent (or one **f-stop**) is referred to as *push one* or *force one*. Film destined for force development must be clearly labeled by the **loader,** as mistaken overprocessing of otherwise normal footage looks bad. Trust me. The actors end up looking like Johnny Winter.

radio mic: Tiny microphones gingerly placed under the actors' clothing by the **sound department**. See **wireless mic**.

Radioman: Bizarre homeless street character (he wears a radio boom box around his neck on a leash) who is well known to all New York film people. Radioman (aka Craig Schwartz) lives off **craft-service** food and spends his time traveling among various movie **sets**, cross-pollinating the **crews** with insider film gossip and entertaining news. "Did you know De Niro's movie across town is going over budget? The **lab** ruined all the film, and they lost two **locations**." *The New Yorker* magazine profiled him a few years back, and Ron Howard bought him a bicycle, increasing his range to include the entire tri-state area. Only in New York.

rag: Any large unframed silk, net, or **flag** used by the **grips** under the direction of the **DP** to control the light. The rags are stored on the grip truck in clearly labeled bags, ready to be deployed at a moment's notice.

rain deflector: Water hitting the front of the **lens** can make your **feature** movie look like it was filmed underwater by Jacques Cousteau. A high-rpm spinning disc of clear glass can be fitted to the front of the **camera** to fling off raindrops. Just make sure you use it only around pure, clear rainwater. On *Scent of a Woman,* we tried to use a spinning rain deflector on dripping milk during one scene, and ended up with faces full of whipped cream. Not good.

rain effect: Light rain falling from the heavens often can't be seen by the movie film, so if a particular **scene** calls for rain, we make our own. Water trucks or fire hydrants pump water to hoses and artfully disguised pipe towers, and the ensuing deluge is then **backlit** for maximum visibility. If you need even more water, you can add big containers of water called dump tanks, or monster hoses called water cannons. I've never been so wet, cold, and miserable as when filming rain shots on the Dutch killer elevator film *Down*. Don't forget the **workday** is twelve hours long. On the other hand, when the **director** yells, "Cut!" the rain instantly stops as if by magic.

rainpants: What the **crew** wears over their street clothes when we're creating **rain effect**. Later, you can strip off the wet layer and emerge from your cocoon completely dry. Just don't leave your shirt-tail hanging out of your open fly, like yours truly did when meeting big shot **producer-director** Ridley Scott on the set of *Black Rain*.

rate: How much you're paid for a day's work, expressed in relation to the number of hours worked, such as two hundred dollars for eight, or six hundred dollars for ten, and so forth. Each person on a movie can individually negotiate the rate of pay, though a **union** may have a **scale rate**, or on non-union jobs, a **street rate** might prevail. Long **workdays** (twelve to sixteen hours) are the norm, so don't forget about overtime. One exception is **stuntmen** who are often paid for each **take**. (Hey, would *you* jump off a burning building for just five hundred dollars?)

raw stock: Film that hasn't yet been through the camera. Manu-factured by Kodak or Fuji, raw stock comes in large rolls in factory-sealed in metal cans, secured with a piece of white tape. A can is roughly the size of a dinner plate and holds four hundred to a thousand feet of tightly spooled film. Open only in a **darkroom**, please.

reaction shot: Simply put, a **shot** of an **actor** who's listening. Early movie audiences felt cheated unless they got to see Barrymore's or Clark Gable's every utterance, but we've now evolved to the point where a modern film or TV show contains dozens to hundreds of reaction shots. Shakespeare on a stage is a drama of **dialogue,** but film stories are told through dialogue and reaction. And car chases.

reader: A person employed by a **director, producer**, or **studio** specifically to read the many scripts offered to them by struggling writers. By delegating this activity to readers, producers can sort through all the potentially good movie projects, and claim ignorance if they happen to inadvertently "borrow" some ideas.

rear projection: This is when a **background** for a **set** is projected onto a screen behind the **actors**, and the **camera** out front records the resulting combined shot. The background is also called the **plate**. See **process**.

recan: Film that has been put into a **mag** but not yet run through the **camera** is often recanned by the **loader**. After **principal photography** is complete, the producer might collect these **short ends** for resale, unless crew members have squirreled them away for use on their own upcoming projects.

redhead: Not Lucille Ball or Molly Ringwald, *redhead* is slang for a thousand-watt light, the smaller brother of the **blonde**. Also called a **mickey** (aka mickey mole), these units are used for many purposes, such as creating a streetlight effect at night or coupling to a **chimera** to make a **softlight**. They're small, so you can usually plug them directly into **house** power, making them a favorite of **gaffers** on low-budget films.

reel: (1) See **demo reel**. Trying to land a job in **special effects** at DreamWorks? Show them your reel.

(2) A film ready for **projection** is divided into several reels, there being a limit to the size of film rolls the movie projector at the local **cineplex** can handle.

reference tone: The **sound mixer** lays down a special beep on the **soundtrack** at the beginning of each sound **roll** to help the many other soundtrack artists later calibrate their machines. "This is sound roll number 365 of the film *Big Daddy* recorded on June 10, with a negative ten-decibel reference tone coming up right now. . . . *Beeeeeeeeeep!*"

reflector: Shiny silver or gold lamé material affixed to a board can be used to reflect sunlight. Advantage—it takes no electricity or setup time. Disadvantage—if Mr./Mrs. **Movie Star** comes to the set even a few minutes late, chances are the sun has moved or gone behind a cloud, and you'll need to frantically direct the **crew** to fire up some artificial movie lights.

rehearsal: Acting the **scene**, moving the **camera** around, executing the lighting **cues**, all without actually flipping on the camera switch. Broadway plays might rehearse for weeks on end, but in the magical (and expensive) world of the movies, rehearsing is minimal. If the actors have simply memorized the **dialogue**, the **director** might say "Let's shoot the rehearsal!" Hoo-wah!

release print: The final version of the film that gets shipped to the multiplex cinema for **projection**. These days two thousand to three thousand release prints are made of each film, in a coordinated effort by the **producers** and **studios** to cash in on the big opening **weekend**. But make one little bootleg DVD, and watch 'em turn you over to the feds!

reload: Film **cameras** hold one thousand feet, or roughly ten minutes, of film. When the film runs out, the 1st **AC** says loudly, "Camera reloads!" This tells the **loader** to hand over a fresh roll of film, and everyone else that there will be a short pause. All eyes are on the 1st AC as he or she threads the film through the camera. Nothing much will happen until they give the okay. Time for **last looks**.

remote head: Large manned **Hollywood** camera **cranes**, swooping over the **backlot**, have given way to smaller, lighter, remote-control camera systems. The smaller payload (no one rides at the end of the arm) makes for more dynamic and interesting moving shots. Check out the films of **DP** Roger Deakins (*O Brother, Where Art Thou?* and *The Shawshank Redemption)* for examples of great remote head **shots**.

rental house: Expensive **cameras**, **grip** equipment, and **movie lights** are too expensive for a short-term purchase by most film **productions**, so all the necessary gear is rented by the day or week. Rental houses such as **Panavision**, Camera Service Center, Otto Nemenz, and Clairmont Camera are where you will find the camera gear between **shows**. Getting a job at one of these is a good way to get some hands-on training with high-tech gear and to hear about upcoming projects.

reshoot: Often movies **shoot** additional material after a **rough cut** is completed, and the reasons may surprise you: (1) Often there are no real mistakes to fix, but when trimmed to ninety minutes, the film makes no sense. A bridging **scene** is then subsequently photographed, and the main characters sit around a dinner table describing the (missing) **plot** developments. (2) **Close-ups** missed during **principal photography** due to time constraints. (3) A chance to redo the ending after the audience walks out during **previews**.

residuals: Money from a percentage of a film's "profits," which trickle down years after its release to those **actors**, **directors**, and **crew** people smart enough to negotiate for them. The popularity of DVD sales has greatly increased residual payments in recent years. Now **producers** will go to great lengths to avoid residual obligations; for example, George Lucas reportedly shot *Star Wars, Episode 3* in England and Australia in order to avoid paying residuals in accordance with the **SAG** contract covering the United States. See **runaway production**.

Ridefilm: This is a company name and term coined by **Oscar**-winning **special effects** wizard Douglas Trumbull for expensive special-venue films shown to audiences strapped into moving chairs in theme parks, such as *Back to the Future: The Ride* and *Luxor*. These are generally short, because tests indicate that the violent motion will cause most people to lose their lunches if the film goes on for more than a few minutes.

rig: A bunch of **grip** or **camera** hardware dedicated to getting a particular **shot**, or the act of setting up such a contraption. The **Steadicam** operator's personal gear is his rig. To set up **movie lights**

over a swimming pool is to rig the lights. To mount the camera to a car in preparation for shooting *The Dukes of Hazzard Return!* is to set up the **car rig**.

rigger: This refers to **stunt coordinators, electrics,** or **grips** hired especially to build or assemble movie support equipment. No real federal- or state-level certification is required, just a good track record of not dropping stuff on people's heads.

rimlight: This is a **backlight** placed above and behind an **actor**, often to highlight their hair.

riser: An extension for the **tripod, crane,** or **dolly** that makes the camera taller for a particular shot. In a daring slang experiment, I've tried to introduce the phrase *BAR,* short for *big-ass riser* on movie **sets,** but only time will tell if this one sticks. I'll let you know how it turns out.

ritter fan: This is one of those "only in **Hollywood**" pieces of gear used all the time on films. Giant wooden propeller blades are mounted on a discarded auto or plane engine and set on a **trailer,** which is used as a fan. A really *big* fan. Need a tornado for *Wizard of Oz II: Return of the Cowardly Lion*? Rent a couple of ritters. Just be sure to **sandbag** the lights.

roach coach: Derogatory term for the **caterer's** truck. That's not fair. All told, I've enjoyed many first-class gourmet meals, all provided by the **producer** for free on movie **sets** around the world. Then again, sometimes I bring a PB&J from home in a paper bag.

roll sound: The words spoken by the **assistant director** to commence filming. The sound **mixer** working with various machines stacked on the **sound cart** needs a few seconds to get things moving. When ready, he tells the **boom operator**, who then yells **"speed,"** the **camera operator** turns on the camera, the **slate** is clapped, and *then* the **director** calls **"Action!"** The whole process takes from three to ten seconds, and serves as a nice ramp-up to filming.

room tone: Not the atmosphere of a dinner club. Each film **location** has its own individual sound character (Carnegie Hall sounds different from Fifty-seventh Street outside), so after completing the real job of shooting a **scene**, the entire **crew** freezes in place and remains perfectly still and quiet for an additional thirty seconds of blank sound recording. Also referred to as **ambience**. The **editor** mixes in these bits of blank room tone to smooth over minute differences in sound **takes**.

Rotoscope: At one time this was the time-consuming and expensive process by which a second photographic element is combined with the original image, after the fact. Replacing the picture on a TV set, having a steamship appear in the crosshairs of a pair of binoculars—these used to be classic Rotoscope shots, but are now more easily achieved using computers.

rough cut: The first complete edited version of the film, normally ready about one month after **principal photography** is completed. It's the rough cut because the **producers** and the **studio** big shots in charge of spending money might feel a little "rough." Don't worry, Mr. Producer . . . wait until after all the **foley** sound, **special effects**, and **reshoots** have been added. Supposedly, the **Oscar**-winning film *Chariots of Fire* was nearly unwatchable until the driving musical score by Vangelis was added at the last minute.

rubber lens: Derogatory term. See **zoom**.

run lines: When **actors** get together and practice saying their **dialogue,** without a lot of moving around and "acting."

run of the picture: When the **producers** want to make sure a particular **actor** or **crew** person is available to work on a daily basis throughout **principal photography** (four to twenty weeks), they will hire them for the run of the picture. **Call time** tomorrow . . . 6 a.m.

run over: When a **feature** film falls behind schedule and additional shooting days are needed to complete **principal photography,** the film is said to run over. This can create problems because of **actor availability** or budgetary constraints (running out of money . . . see **bond company.**)

runaway production: This is a relatively new term that describes movies **shot** abroad by their cheap **producers** in an attempt to save some money. Movies set in New York can be shot in Toronto, where government subsidies have fueled a resurgent film economy. Likewise, **commercials** can be filmed with low-wage English-speaking  actors in Australia or South Africa to avoid paying **residuals** to American **actors**. This has resulted in decreased work opportunities and lost jobs for American actors and **crews,** but the profit-driven laws of supply and demand affect **Hollywood** as well as Wall Street. Movies, like sneakers, compact cars, and television sets, can be less expensive to manufacture abroad.

running shot: This doesn't involve an **actor** running through the streets, but rather a **thespian** behind the wheel, driving a car. Clear the streets.

running time: The exact number of minutes between "A long time ago, in a land far, far away . . ." and THE END. The running time for a **feature** film was once around ninety minutes, though these days it seems to be getting longer. Maybe it's my attention span that's getting shorter. Probably both.

rushes: See **dailies**. This is footage filmed the previous day returned to the **production** in a hurry from the **lab** or the **film-to-tape** transfer.

SAG: Screen Actors Guild. Anyone can qualify for membership once they have appeared in a movie. SAG is a well-run, powerful **union**. (Any actor you can name is a member.) They oversee contracts and working conditions on all SAG films and have quite a good health plan for members who work the required minimum number of days each year. Of course, you're not allowed to be in films made by the major studios unless you're *already* in SAG. Catch-22.

sandbag: Lots of heavy canvas bags filled with sand are used by the **grips** to hold down the various lighting stands and equipment. Smaller bags are often filled with lead or steel shot, and are referred to as shotbags. No need to join an expensive health club—there's plenty of heavy gear to move around right on the movie **set**!

scale: The minimum **rate** of daily pay as dictated by **union** contract. Clever **producers** will get **crew** members to work at or near published scale rates, and often budgets on smaller **independent films** become viable only if they're able to convince the expensive **actors** to work for **SAG** scale. They then offer the actors a **back-end** deal consisting of a share of anticipated future profits. . . . Ha! And the Chicago Cubs will win the World Series.

scene: A collection of several **shots** with a common **theme**, filmed generally at one **location**. Purists might argue that some movie scenes consist of just one shot (the **one-er** to the working crew).

scout: The act of looking for **locations** appropriate for filming. Scouting can be a simple walk down the street by the **DP** looking for a nice angle, or a trip by all key personnel in the **crew van**. Essential gear for any scout includes a **Polaroid** or digital **camera**, a watch, and a compass. With some advance planning, you can ensure that the sunset in your epic film will take place over the anticipated "mountain vista," and not a sewage-treatment plant.

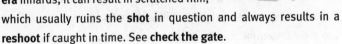

scratch: If a tiny, tiny loose chip of film **emulsion** is caught inside the movie **camera** innards, it can result in scratched film, which usually ruins the **shot** in question and always results in a **reshoot** if caught in time. See **check the gate**.

scratchtrack: Same as **guide track**. This is a substandard recording of the **actors' dialogue**, or a music **temp track** used to fill space in the edited film until **ADR** or rerecording is complete.

screen direction: See also **cross the line**. When filming car chases, shoot-outs, and the like, the **director** creates a believable world by having the good guys shoot their guns all pointing to the left, and the bad guys shooting to the right, for example. When **editing** the various angles, a coherent **narrative** is created, but only if the director maintains proper screen direction. Every **shot** in a film has to dovetail with the shots coming before and after.

screen time: One of the tricks to good narrative fiction filmmaking is keeping straight the difference in real time and the fictional movie time. For example, we filmed the Jet Ski **scene** for the Will Smith movie *Hitch* on four separate days, spread out over three months. In screen time, the scene is meant to take place in about thirty minutes. All the costumes, makeup, hairstyles, and lighting need to match as closely as possible over the course of those four different **shoot** days to maintain **continuity**.

screening room: This can be synonymous with movie theater. Film **lab** screening rooms are used by the **director**, **editor**, **producer**, and the **DP** for projecting and checking **prints** during the period of **postproduction**.

screenplay: This is the hundred-page written text containing all the **dialogue** and **action**; it serves as the template for shooting the movie. A great original screenplay is hard to find—witness the tendency of producers to adapt best-selling novels, existing Broadway shows, and even comic books, rather than to develop new ideas. Don't get me wrong, there are plenty of screenplays circulating out there, just a scarcity of original ones.

screenwriter: Special breed of fiction prose stylist who is able to write in hundred-page bursts of **dialogue**, humor, and descriptive **action**, all the while maintaining a **narrative** flow and perhaps offering some insight into the human condition. Not that easy. Many leading novelists have also tried their hand at scriptwriting (William Faulkner, Ben Hecht, William Goldman). Hey, everyone has bills!

scrim: On the Broadway stage, a scrim refers to a large, nearly see-through fabric set backing . . . ah, but who cares about *Broad-*

way? In the wonderful world of motion pictures, a scrim is a small round wire mesh, placed inside a movie light to effectively reduce its output. Scrims (also called wires) come in singles (green = 1/2 stop exposure) and doubles (red = 1 full stop exposure). This will be on the test at the end of the book, so start taking notes.

script: Screenplay. Every **crew** member, film student, and **Holly-wood** wannabe has written one of these in an attempt to draw a producer's attention. (Mine's about an average guy who wins the lottery.) Better work on the **pitch**.

script supervisor: In former, less politically correct days, they were called "script girls." The script supervisor can be seen carrying a giant heavy book around, constantly writing cryptic notes. The **editor** occasionally consults these notes months later during **editing**. The **script** notes describe in detail all the **camera** data, **actor's** movements, as well as all the **lines** spoken in each individual take. If an actor's hairdo flip-flops or the level of wine in a glass changes between takes, it's termed a break in **continuity**. Finding these mistakes in **Hollywood** movies is good fun at home with a DVD player with freeze-frame. Check out Oscar winner Richard Dreyfuss in Neil Simon's film *The Goodbye Girl*. He comes home drunk after receiving some bad play reviews, and promptly knocks over an entire table, complete with flowers, desk lamp—the works. Ten seconds of **screen time** later, the table is back together, the room unchanged. Oops!

seamless: Inexpensive eight-foot-wide rolls of colored construction paper that are commonly used as backdrops for **commercials**, particularly on **product shots**.

second meal: If the **workday** goes past twelve hours, the **producer** may have the caterer serve the working film **crew** a half-hour sit-down meal, six hours after **lunch**. Occasionally, an informal second meal (why is it always pizza?) is provided as a courtesy while the **crew** wraps the gear after a long, hard day.

second second: When an additional **AD** is hired to work under the 2nd **assistant director,** the position is often referred to as the 2nd 2nd. For some reason, there is no 3rd assistant director position. The hierarchy of the on-set production team from the top down is: assistant director, 2nd AD, 2nd 2nd AD, **DGA trainee,** key set PA, **PA, parking PA,** passerby, stranger.

second sticks: When something goes awry, or a person (me) simply forgets to turn on the **camera,** an assistant loudly shouts, "Second sticks!" the **slate** is clapped once more, and off we go. It is a courtesy to shout "second sticks" into the **mic** to help the **editor** synchronize the correct take with the matching correct *clap* sound. See also **endslate.**

second team: See **stand-in.** These are the people who politely stand in front of the hot lights during **setup** time, when the **actors** are **in the works.**

second unit: Big action movies and smaller films falling behind schedule often employ this skeleton **crew** to photograph the needed **inserts, stunts,** and indeed any **shot** without the big movie **stars.** The typical James Bond film uses several second unit crews working simultaneously, often in different countries. On the other hand, smaller-scale New York or L.A. **productions** might simply send three people around in a **crew van** to photograph scenic vistas or **estab-**

lishing shots. This is filmmaking at its very best: no **producers**, no stars, no hassles. Just **cameras** and sunlight.

sequence: A series of **shots** dedicated to exploring one **story point** or a single **theme**, generally consisting of several **scenes**. A car chase and a falling-in-love **montage** are two good examples of sequences.

set: Where the action is. On a multifaceted film **production**, the set is the place where the **camera** is currently filming. This could be someone's living room or a space designed from scratch by the **art director** and built on a **soundstage**. Other important physical spaces involved in produc- tion include the **office**, the **holding area**, and **base camp**.

set decorator: Art department person who hovers over the **set dresser** and decides where to put all the heavy furniture required for the **scene**.

set dresser: While most of the **art department** is off decorating future **locations**, the dresser is left behind and works with the shoot- ing **crew** to rearrange the furniture in the moments just prior to film- ing. The perfect dresser is an artistically inclined weight lifter.

set piece: An extra free-standing section of a **set** wall or ceiling that is available for **inserts**, or hiding lights. Normally the **DP** or **pro- duction designer** will ask for a set piece well in advance of photogra- phy. A last-minute small set piece is sometimes fashioned from an extra shelving board or a piece of **foam core**, and touched up with paint by the **stand-by scenic**.

setup: A setup refers to one particular placement of the movie **camera** and lights. With good planning, sometimes two or three **shots** can be made from a single setup.

shoot: A verb meaning to capture a photographic or video image. *Shoot* also is a noun describing a particular project, as in, "I have an Alpo shoot on Thursday—how's Friday for lunch?"

shooting schedule: Usually this is reworked and printed weekly by the **AD,** to keep all key **crew** personnel in the loop during **principal photography**. However, the **call sheet** goes out to all crew members every day. See also **advance schedule**.

short end: After a **scene** is completed, there may be some unused film left in the camera **mag**. This is recanned and saved by the film **loader,** to be used later, when only a short length of film (one hundred to three hundred feet) is needed. Jim Jarmusch's excellent and very weird first film, *Stranger Than Paradise,* was reportedly shot entirely on short ends left over after another film had wrapped, an artistic use of recycling.

shot: In a finished film, the smallest indivisible unit is the shot: one **camera** showing one angle filmed once. Shots are assembled into completed **scenes,** which of course are edited together to make the finished film.

shot list: An overambitious list detailing the day's intended work is referred to as a *wish list,* though generally not within hearing of the **producer** or **director**. Many directors, **DPs,** and **script supervisors** compile shot lists first thing in the morning to ensure no **camera** angles or **story points** are forgotten once the afternoon rush starts.

Shotmaker: Shotmaker is an excellent brand of large truck, specially designed and built for filming **running shots**. Many have **jib** arms and onboard **gennys** to run movie lights. Add spill-proof cup holders, and they'd be perfect.

show: Short for *TV show,* but in **Hollywood** lingo, *show* is also synonymous with *feature film.* "Sorry, I couldn't **shoot** that Alpo spot last week. I was busy on a show."

show card: It's strange that something as simple as a black-and-white two-by-three-foot piece of cardboard could be essential in the making of a multimillion-dollar film. Dozens of show cards are used to mask imperfections in the **set**, shield the **camera lens** from stray light, write **cue cards,** what have you. Show cards belong to that category of items referred to as **expendables**.

sidelight: Lighting coming from the side of, rather than in front of or behind, the **talent**. This can add strong dramatic shadows to a scene. Okay, in a nutshell, here's the secret to good **Hollywood** lighting—and you had to read almost the whole book to get here: When setting lights, you need to sidelight rain, **frontlight** falling snow and aging movie actresses, and **backlight** everything else. Class dismissed.

sides: Miniature **script** pages prepared by the **production** team and handed out to the **actors** and movie **crew** first thing each morning. Sides are consulted when trying to remember your **lines** (actor) or when trying to **cue** the **mic** (**boom operator**).

silk: Thin diffuse white material placed in front of movie lights by **grips** to create a heavenly glow. Silks can be **flag**-sized, or huge twenty-by-twenty-foot **overheads**, which are rolled up and stored on the **grip** truck.

single: (1) At home you call it an extension cord. Of course, thick movie singles carry a lot of electricity, and they're covered in heavy-duty rubber to make them idiot-proof.

(2) Single is a thin round wire **scrim**, mounted in front of hot movie lamps in order to quickly reduce the intensity of the beam. To avoid mix-ups, the metal edge of a single scrim is color-coded green.

(3) *Single* also refers to a **close-up** shot in which only one **actor** appears. It's customary to first shoot a **master shot** and then "go in for singles" or "go in for **coverage.**"

single camera: Movies are generally photographed one **shot** at a time by a single camera, unlike a multicamera show like *Survivor* or *The Bachelor*. If you think about it, it makes sense. Complete attention can be paid to optimizing lighting and the **actors'** performances for one angle at a time. Matching up all the shots and keeping track of slight variations in **action** and **dialogue** are the province of the **script supervisor.**

slate: A twelve-inch square of Plexiglas (in the old days, it was a slate chalkboard) that lists important information such as the **working title,** the **director,** the **DP, camera roll** number, and so on. The

slate is put in front of the camera at the beginning of a **take,** the scene numbers are verbally called out, and the stick at the top of the slate is clapped. The 2nd **AC** or the **loader** gets to do the honors. The **editor** later synchronizes the film with the **soundtrack** by matching the visual of the **sticks** banging together with the *pop* on the separately recorded soundtrack. These days, a fancy expensive digital device (Smart Slate) is often used, and when the batteries crap out, a handclap in front of the **lens** will suffice.

slug: This is a blank bit of film or sound temporarily inserted as a place-saver into a film being edited, most often while the **editor** is awaiting a FedEx package from **ILM** or another **postproduction** facility.

smoke: I worked on the Miramax film *Smoke,* which was a hit only in Europe, where smokers are unrepentant. When photographing in a bar or a large **interior** space, such as a church, **prop** people may use any number of methods to fill the set with a thin atmospheric haze. It makes things look lovely, but is rough on the lungs of the hardworking **crew**. On another film, I once saw Donald Sutherland refuse to walk onto the **set** until all the prop smoke had been cleared. He then proceeded to light up a cigarette in front of the camera during the **take**! I guess the character he was playing in the film smoked, but he didn't! See **method acting**.

snap zoom: Another **music video** shooting technique that is finding its way into today's action-based **feature** films. The **camera-person frames** up a **shot**, and then cranks hard on the **lens zoom** ring, quickly bringing the **actor** (or exploding car, or whatever) optically much closer.

snoot: A snoot is a black metal tube attached to the front of a movie light to shape or contain the resulting light beam. A heavy-duty lampshade that resembles a stovepipe hat. Common **gaffer** phrase is "Give me a **baby** with a snoot!"

snorkel lift: Huge industrial man-lifts, bucket trucks, and scissor-lifts are often used to hang lights high over a nighttime city street **set**. They're not great for placing **cameras** on high. Better to use a specially built camera **crane** or a **remote head**.

snow effect: Rain is cold, wet, and miserable for the working movie **crew**, but snow is easy. A real snowstorm can be used if the crew works fast. But Mother Nature is undependable when the snow needs to last all day. Then again, maybe you're filming a Jack London story in Burbank. Flakes of cornstarch movie snow can be simply tossed into the air in front of a **ritter fan**, and you're good to go. If you need real snow for a movie, telephone a man named Dieter Sturm (great name!) in Wisconsin. This guy showed up on the **set** of M. Night Shyamalan's film *Wide Awake* in Philadelphia with a big truck filled with ice and a magic snow hose. His crew covered a whole neighborhood with snow (finely chipped ice) in one hour. Turns out he invented the movie cornstarch snow, as well. Did you know that in Wisconsin they have dozens of names for snow?

softlight: The difference between hardlight and softlight can be described as the difference between a sunny day and a cloudy day. The gentle shadowless lighting of a cloudy day is great for photographing **close-ups** of people. This is the time to get that great picture of your grandmother. Several types of movie lights are designed with large white reflecting surfaces in order to provide this pleasing soft light.

sound blankets: Better known to the U-Haul-renting public as furniture pads, these thick pleated and stitched blankets are laid on the floor or hung about the **set** in an attempt to **kill** extraneous noise. They have many other uses, among them protecting innocent bystanders while using **squibs**, and padding out **apple boxes** for seating comfort.

sound cart: This is the portable wheeled conveyance holding all the **mixer's** sound recorders, **boom poles**, **cables**, and microphones. When it's time for **moving on**, the sound crew will simply wheel the cart in place for the next **shot**, generally placing it fifteen to twenty feet behind the camera. Naturally.

sound department: The two or three people whose job it is to hold the **mics**, place the audio **cables**, and run the sound recording equipment. Additionally, they're often called upon to hide tiny microphones on a movie **star's** person, under their clothing. Excuse me, Jamie Lee, just doing my job!

sound designer: As distinct from the sound **mixer**, who records the **actors' dialogue** live on **set**. These folks work during **postproduction** in small dark rooms, piecing together tiny bits of sounds, **effects**, and music, long after the glamour of shooting the film is over.

sound effects: Gunshots, lion roars, horse hoofbeats, explosions . . . these sounds are added to the film weeks after the completion of **principal photography**. Some movie sound effects might actually seem more realistic to our ears than the real thing. For example, gunshots on the street never make the Old West whining ricochet-off-a-boulder sound; they sound like a dull pop. (Hey, I live in New York!) But that's not good for the movies, so **foley** editors usually **mix** in a few ricochets for "realism."

soundstage: The reason this is called a soundstage, and not a film stage, is the importance of recording a nice clean, quiet **dialogue soundtrack** during filming. We want to hear the movie **stars**. Music, explosions, **foley** sounds, and the like are added later during **postproduction**, but care is still taken to obtain a quality soundtrack while shooting. Requirements for a soundstage are a giant **interior** space, high ceilings, and good electrical power.

sound transfer: The **actor's dialogue** is originally recorded on a hard drive, a DAT (digital audiotape), or quarter-inch tape on a **Nagra** and must be dubbed to different formats for editing and release purposes (miniDV, digital file, D2, Digi-beta, MP3—you name it, it's been done). This sound transfer is normally done overnight while the film is being processed by the **lab**, so that the two elements (sound and picture) might be reunited in time for **dailies**.

soundtrack: (1) The big difference between a silent movie and a "talkie." During **principal photography**, *soundtrack* refers to the **actor's** spoken **dialogue** recorded live on **set**.

(2) During **editing**, *soundtrack* also refers to all the sounds taken from various sources, **dialogue**, music, **foley**, and **effects**, which make up the completed sound portion of a movie.

(3) A third use of the word *soundtrack* is the CD album of popular music that often accompanies the release of many hit films. Occasionally, this soundtrack CD makes more money than the film, such as any film starring Mariah Carey, Whitney Houston, or Britney Spears.

source lighting: This is a particular style of lighting, actually the only style that makes sense. If you walk into a bar and a single flickering lamp is dangling over the pool table, then this is the "look" you should try to emulate with your movie lights when creating a bar scene. The original source of the light serves as the guide.

sparks: Across the pond in England, electricians are called sparks, and are responsible for lighting work as well as the functions usually performed in the USA by **grips**.

special business extra: Not just an **extra** or a **dayplayer**, but an **actor** who's been coached by the **director** and performs a specific action during a **scene**. You see them listed in the credits as Man on Telephone or Soldier #1, and they receive a **bump** in pay for their fine efforts.

special effects: (1) The on-**set** rain, **smoke**, explosions, and the like are referred to as *special effects* during **principal photography**. Likewise, the people who deliver the rain, smoke, and explosions, ready for filming on **cue**, belong to a **department** called special effects.

(2) During **postproduction** *special effects* refers to the model, composite, and computer-generated **shots** that might be needed to enhance the director's vision of the film.

special effects makeup artist: The person who makes the rubber ape mask or fat suit for the lead **actor** has a chance at winning an individual gold statue come **Oscar** time.

speed: On **set**, the word *speed* is the sound **crew's** reply to the **AD's** command "**Roll sound!**" instead of the more logical "Ready!" It means the machines are on, the sound is being recorded, and the crew is . . . ready. In other words, everything's up to speed.

speed rail: The **grips** use pieces of long two-inch-diameter aluminum tubing, fastened together temporarily, to put **cameras** on cars, build frames for **overheads**, and to secure **parallels**. The pipes assemble together and break down quickly, hence the name. Time is money, so movie **shoots** employ modular construction.

splinter unit: A SWAT team called in to remove small pieces of wood from a movie **star** who's been sitting on **apple boxes**. But seriously, when falling behind schedule, planned **shots** may have to be scrapped, or a small ad hoc **second unit** consisting of two to eight people can be left behind to **shoot** the needed **inserts**.

splits: This is when the **workday** starts at noon (yeah!) but continues until midnight (boo!). The **shooting schedule** calls for both day and night shots. Scheduling a day or two of splits midweek can help transition the groggy film **crew** between day and nighttime shooting schedules.

spring clamp: Giant metal clothespin-type fastener. Many popular hardware store items find their way onto the movie **set**, and into my car trunk at **wrap**.

spritzer: A spritzer is a pump bottle of water used for misting the **actor's** skin or clothing so that it appears wet or shiny. (Think Bruce Willis in *Die Hard*.) This provides a realistic substitute for hard-earned sweat, and comes in little Evian bottles imported from France. This raises the question "what do French movie **crews** use?" Poland Spring?

squib: A small battery-powered charge that is rigged on an **actor** or on a **set piece** by the **special effects crew** to provide bullet "hits" or blood splats. See any current popular **Hollywood** film. Films like *The Matrix* and *Terminator 2* are squib-city. No matter how cool and realistically violent a movie seems, remember, live firearms are *never used in filming*. It's all pretend, you guys.

stagebox: Larger studio version of the **lunch box**, a large square electrical distribution box.

staging: (1) When used by the **director** or the **actors**, this means the **blocking** for a particular scene.

(2) When used by a **crew** person, this means the backstage place where all the extra equipment is to be stored between **shots**. Most lighting, **grip**, **prop**, and **camera** gear is kept on rolling carts in a staging area for ease of access. "Bring me a **baby** on a **pigeon!**"

stand-by scenic: The standard movie **crew** includes a painter, re-ferred to as the stand-by painter or the scenic artist. Their job is to stand by, ready to touch up the **set** with paint, wax, and sprays of all kinds. The **DP** might ask the scenic to darken distractingly bright **props**, mist shiny parked cars with **dulling spray**, and even paint shadows onto a wall.

stand-in: Not exactly the same as a **body double**, **stunt double**, or **photo double**. Contrary to that *Seinfeld* episode where Kramer gets work as a stand-in, they rarely recite the **actor's lines**. Stand-ins must simply be exactly the same height and hair color as the **star**. This aids the **DP** in setting up **shots** and planning the lighting, and allows the **actors** to remain off **set**, learning their lines. The stand-ins mirror the actors' movements established during the **blocking re-hearsal** and are sometimes called the **second team**.

star: Self-explanatory. Having met hundreds of **actors** and movie stars, I can say they fall into two groups: regular nice folks like you and me, and big jerks (thankfully, quite rare). They often start in obscurity as dramatic **actors**, dedicated to a demanding craft. Soon they begin longing for fame and fortune, and once they've achieved celebrity, most of them just want to be left alone all over again! (No pic-tures! Please, Mr. Pitt needs his privacy!) It must be a great job, being a movie star—pre-tending to be someone else, playing dress-up,

lots of money, international travel, adoring fans, lots of money. Where do I sign up?

Steadicam: Developed by **Oscar**-winning inventor Garrett Brown in the mid-1970s, this is a body harness and **camera** contraption with which an **operator** walks or runs, all the time delivering **dolly**-smooth pictures. It was first used on the movies *Bound for Glory* and *Rocky*. Steadicam has since become wildly popular, contributing gliding shots to all kinds of TV shows and movies, from *ER* to the Super Bowl. My greatest Steadicam **shot** is when I chased Jodie Foster through the maze at the beginning of *The Silence of the Lambs*. I ran hard and kept up fairly well—we're roughly the same age—only at the time I had seventy pounds of camera gear strapped to my back!

Steadicam operator: A chiropractor's best client; see above. Steadicam operators generally command a premium salary and spend tons of time and money maintaining their custom **rigs**. The original Steadicam specialist, Garrett Brown, was smart enough to train a legion of **operators** who have followed in his very large footsteps.

sticks: (1) A **tripod**, sometimes used for stationary shots instead of a **dolly**. "Set up the sticks, hurry!"

(2) *Sticks* can also refer to the **slate**, or the act of slating. "Clap the sticks, hurry!" These movie people are always in such a hurry.

still photographer: A still photographer is usually hired daily to shoot behind-the-scenes pictures of the **stars** and also to document the **director** and **crew** at work. They're hired by the **publicist** and are distinct from the annoying **paparazzi**.

stock shot: This is film footage that has been previously photographed and stockpiled by someone else and is purchased by the **producer** in an effort to save money. Using stock images is quite common in picture magazines, TV **shows**, and **commercials**, but for **feature** films, it's often more expedient to dispatch a **second unit**.

stop motion: *The Gumby Show* and the Wallace & Gromit films are made with stop-motion **animation** techniques: You take a picture, *stop*. Move the clay figure, take a picture, *stop*. And so forth. *Stop*.

story point: This is a bit of **business**, a **prop**, a thematic element, or specific **dialogue** around which the **plot** turns. For example, when Ingrid Bergman draws a gun on Humphrey Bogart toward the end of *Casablanca*, the camera **tilts** down to show the gun, underscoring a story point. (She has a gun!) It's the **director's** primary job to keep all the story points in mind, and to ensure they make it to the screen. Well, that and coaching the **actors**.

storyboard artist: Before **principal photography** starts, an artist may draw the pictures representing the film, which the **director** might use to plan his **shots**. Fine artistry is less of a job prerequisite than understanding how complex movie **scenes** break down into individual shots and how **cameras** interpret things.

storyboards: Little cartoon pictures that act as templates for shooting the film. Some very good **directors** always use them; others never do. Filmmakers often use boards to convince the **studio** that they have a good handle on how to visually tell the story. **Scenes** heavy with action and **special effects** are always storyboarded, as surprise outcomes are rarely appreciated when **stunts** are involved. On **commercials**, the **crew** posts the storyboards on the wall at the beginning of the day and crosses off the finished individual **shots** with a marker as the day progresses. One down—thirty-seven to go!

straight-to-video: Ever wonder about all those thousands of titles at the video store? "Look, honey, another cop-murder-mystery with Morgan Freeman!" Well, when a film doesn't warrant a widespread **theatrical release**, it will nevertheless soon find its way to local video outlets in an attempt to recoup some portion of the investors' money.

street rate: The informal unpublished going rate of daily pay for a particular movie **crew** position, often more than the minimum called for by the union **scale** rate.

strike: (1) A simple work stoppage originating with disgruntled employees, the opposite of an employer lockout. Let's remember that in the days of sailing and exploration, rebelling crews would band together, mutiny, and take over the whole ship.

(2) *Strike* most commonly is the term used when you want something removed from the **set**, as in "Strike the **redhead**, we're ready to roll!" Synonyms for *strike it* include *lose it, 86 it,* **FO**, *adios it,* and *it's toast*.

strike the baby and kill the blonde: The title of this book when translated means, "Please, sir, remove the small spotlight from the **set**, and kindly switch off the two-kilowatt quartz light." Not quite so catchy when you say it that way.

strobing: From *stroboscopic*. If you fully understand this term, you're well on your way to unlocking the technical secrets of the

Panavision camera. Films (not videos) photograph twenty-four individual **frames** each second, at a shutter speed of 1/48 second. Still with me? If the camera or **actor** moves laterally at a fast rate of speed, there will be some blurring of the image, or strobing. See also **whip pan**.

studio: This is a commercial space dedicated to shooting film, but more important, a slang name for the big-money bosses overseeing your film from L.A. "Call the studio—tell them we got the first shot of the day, 8:23 a.m.!"

stunt: What a trained **stunt player** will do for money, which most normal people try to avoid in daily life: crashing cars, fisticuffs, jumping off buildings while on fire. When do **stars** perform their own stunts? *Never.* That's right. The **bond company** and the insurance people won't let them. Contrary to whatever actors say on *Entertainment Tonight,* Jackie Chan is the only major star who puts himself in harm's way. And he also has a delicious line of herbal beverages that are best-sellers in Hong Kong!

stunt coordinator: Generally a **stuntman** who has wisely decided to supervise **stunts** rather than actually perform them. The stunt coordinator is the ultimate safety authority on the **set**, outranking the **AD**, the **key grip**, and even the **director**! He or she is the one who calls **"Action!"** during all stunts, and nothing happens in front of a film **camera** that is the least bit dangerous without their approval.

stunt double: When a **stunt person** closely resembles a particular **star**, they could have a career "doubling" him or her. Of course, you may be asked to crash cars and jump from buildings in an actor's place, so think carefully before accepting any assignment as a stunt double.

stunt gaffer: A West Coast term for a **stunt coordinator**, often one charged with preparing **stunts,** and not related to the chief electrician, who is the **gaffer.**

stunt man/woman/player: They're handsomely rewarded for doing the seemingly and sometimes truly dangerous things we love to photograph. They're paid for *each take.* Most stunt players wisely aim to graduate to the ranks of **stunt coordinator** before their nine lives run out.

subjective angle: Slightly different from a **POV.** (Listen up, film students!) A subjective angle is a **shot** that represents the viewpoint of a particular person in the film. A swirling drunken camera or a binocular shot (those cheesy shots with crosshairs superimposed) are two good examples.

sugar glass: Breakable glass that shatters easily and yet doesn't cut people is used on movies, and it is actually made of sugar. You can eat the stuff. It's expensive and, compared with real glass, slightly yellow. Just before filming a **stunt,** the **props crew** will switch the real windows for sugar glass.

the suits: I get a charge out of seeing those old black-and-white movie still photos of Hitchcock and his entire movie **crew**—even **grips**—wearing suits, ties, and hats. Forget about hats; these days it's hard enough keeping clean T-shirts and blue jeans on most film people. The only people who occasionally wear suits on a working set are big-shot **executive producers** and dandy movie-star **agents** from L.A.

sun gun: Not *stun gun.* This is a handheld, battery-powered movie light, popular on low-budget films and on larger **Hollywood**

films where no other electrical power source is available. Better to rent a **genny**.

sunset grad: The **script** calls for a sunset, but you don't want to wait for that pesky sun to go down? Throw one of these specialized **filters** in front of the **lens**, and presto! Sunset! Just don't overdo it or your film will look like a Jerry Bruckheimer production shot in Marrakech.

sunshade: This is a small rubber hood that clips on the front of the **camera lens**, shielding it from **flare**. Consider it a smaller and more portable version of the **mattebox**.

swing gang: This sounds like a bunch of ballroom dancers turned into street hoods for a Gap **commercial**, but it is actually two or three people from the **art department** loose on the town, frantically shopping for **props** and furniture.

tableau: This word occasionally finds its way into the vocabulary of some **directors** and highfalutin **production designers**. It means "all the stuff I'm looking at in front of me." For an even fancier term, see **mise-en-scène**.

taco cart: All the **flags, grip stands**, and **apple boxes** are arranged onto huge wheeled contraptions dubbed taco carts. There is no food on them, though; that's at **craft service**. Essential equipment is kept within reach, and the carts can easily be rolled out of view to a new **staging area** if necessary.

take: One individual running of the camera, a single execution of a single **shot**. Many film **actors** love to do multiple takes, crafting a performance through repetition (Al Pacino, Kevin James). On the other hand, a few actors (Anthony Hopkins, James Woods) might deliver a great performance spontaneously on take number one. The technical **crew** needs to be fully rehearsed and ready to capture this lightning in a bottle.

take five: In the **Hollywood** cliché, the **director** needs to chill out a prima donna **star**, so he calls, "Take five!" The **crew** stops whatever they're doing and walks away for a smoke break. In my twenty years of moviemaking, I have never once heard this phrase on the **set**, nor have I ever actually taken five.

talent: Refers exclusively to the people appearing in front of the camera. The **director** or the **DP** may wish the term includes them, but when the **AD** barks, "We need the talent," this means "Fetch the actors."

tape: Without tape, you couldn't make movies, simple as that. Masking tape, **camera** tape, black two-inch paper tape, **gaffer's tape**—they all have their uses. Sticky gray gaffer's tape secures **cables**, affixes rugs to floors, hangs **teasers**. Black paper tape is used to hide **set** imperfections and to reduce glare off shiny surfaces. White camera tape can be used for labeling the **mags**, putting **marks** on the floor, and is excellent for stopping a bleeding cut. Now get back to work!

TBD: When the **production manager**, the **AD**, and the **director** can't decide when or how to photograph a **scene**, they defer the decision and list it on the **call sheet** as TBD—to be decided. When? When they figure it out, that's when!

teamsters: The men who drive the trucks. Between the **load-in** in the morning and driving to a **bonded lot** at night, there is not much for them to do all day, leaving them free to offer witty commentary on your work, the film project, and the state of the world in general. They are surprisingly well paid, but then again, it's not that easy to parallel-park a tandem tractor-trailer on a crowded city street.

teaser: Not a young starlet being chased around the **casting couch**. A teaser is a piece of black **Duvatyne** fabric, a large **flag**, or a piece of painted set that is lowered from above to hide movie lights, create shadows, or to shield the **lens** from **flares**.

tech down: This one's bizarre. Sometimes white colors on fabrics look too white for movie cameras, so **costume designers** and art people have been known to soak white shirts, drapes, and the like in a weak solution of Lipton tea. This makes them appear bright, but not too "hot." Drink **coffee** at **craft service** instead of the new big jug of iced tea.

tech scout: This is a visit via **crew van** to a potential film **location** by the **DP, gaffer, transportation captain, UPM,** and **key grip** to finalize lighting and production planning.

technical advisor: Someone expert in a particular field paid to offer advice during filming. For example, retired New York police detective Bill Clark makes sure Sipowicz and company act like real cops when arresting bad guys on *NYPD Blue.*

technical director: The right hand of the TV **director** on a live **multicamera** video **shoot,** the TD organizes and executes all the requests (commands) of the director, such as "Go to camera 3!" "Cue **talent!**" and "Get my car!"

Technicolor: An early process (circa 1930) that photographed movies in full color by utilizing three huge **Mitchell** cameras shooting simultaneously. Today Technicolor is a film and video **lab** still in business that processes film and makes **release prints** worldwide from facilities in New York, Los Angeles, Rome, and London.

telegraph: When an **actor** slightly flinches just before receiving a pretend punch, he is said to be telegraphing. The **stunt coordinator,**

director, and **camera operator** all watch closely for signs of telegraphing, which might then necessitate **reshoots**.

telephoto: The opposite of **wide-angle**, telephoto lenses bring
distant objects visually closer. Long-**focal-length** telephoto lenses also
introduce a compressed perspective, and can make actors and actresses appear thinner and more attractive (attention—trade secret!). They're also great for getting **close-up** shots while remaining
safely distant, as when filming sports and car crashes.

teleprompter: A big, heavy electronic contraption, mounted in
front of the camera, that feeds the **script** to actors and newscasters
with short-term memory problems. Actually, they're never used on
feature films, since there is plenty of time to **run lines**. Network news
shows and political campaigns are another story, and this is where
the teleprompter shines.

temp track: Editors often utilize "borrowed" music sources on
a temporary basis. Perhaps the composer hasn't finished the musical score yet, and a preview is imminent. (Films always seem
better with music.) Also, negotiations with pop stars and publish-
ers for the rights to use their hit songs might still be in progress.

ten-one: This is polite **walkie-talkie** lingo for, "The person in
question might be found in the restroom." *Ten—one hundred* is cop-
talk for a toilet-oriented refreshment pause.

ten-twenty: Code for "exact location." "What's your ten-twenty?"
when spoken into a **walkie** is cop and movie slang for "Where are
you?"

theatrical release: This is the goal of every **producer**, the exhibition of their film project across the country in darkened movie houses. Of the roughly one thousand feature movies shot every year in the USA, only about three hundred make it to the **cineplex**. For the rest, it's **straight to video**.

theme: (1) What a movie is about in purely descriptive terms. For example, the literal **plot** of *Jaws* (or what happens) is: A shark terrorizes a beach community, eating people and threatening everyone's summer. The theme, however, is: Everyone questions the unknown, and yet sometimes we must face our greatest fears, perhaps finding ourselves in the bargain.

(2) The theme is also the name given to the signature song or melody of the film from the **soundtrack**.

thespian: If you saw *My Big Fat Greek Wedding*, you realize everything originated in Greece, and acting was no exception. *Thespian* is a high-class name for an **actor** or **actress**, named after Thespis, a Greek dramatist who lived around two thousand years ago.

throwaway line: See **aside**. When an actor whispers or delivers a line sotto voce. Latin again!

tie-in: (1) In advertising, this is the practice of bombarding the unwary consumer with tons of promotional stuff from all sides. (Batman cups, Batman T-shirts, Batman music videos, and, oh yeah, Batman movies.)

(2) On a movie **set**, when renting a **genny** is inconvenient or expensive, the **gaffer** will take the cover off a house or building elec-

trical service panel and attach huge copper **cables** to run the **company's** lights and equipment. Of course, the homeowner's electric bill goes up by about a thousand dollars.

tilt: When the **camera operator** changes the camera angle from looking up to down, or vice versa, this is called a *tilt*. Whereas a **pan** is a **shot** moving from side to side (showing a *pan*orama), tilt is a shot moving vertically. This will be on the test.

time permitting: A polite scheduling euphemism for "never." Additional **shots** or entire **scenes** not absolutely essential for advancing the **plot** of the film are noted at the bottom of the **call sheet** as "time permitting." As the normal afternoon filming panic sets in, it soon becomes obvious that there is only just barely time to film the most important shots. Time-permitting shots are rarely even attempted.

timing: The **lab** process of adjusting the exposure and color of a completed film by repeated **printing**, viewing, note taking, and reprinting. This is performed by the **DP**, aided by the lab's **color timer** prior to a film's **theatrical release**.

Titan: A Titan is a brand of specialized **camera crane** made in **Hollywood** by Chapman and is one of the best ways to mount a big **Panavision** camera and two full-figured camerapeople on the end of a moving **boom** arm. It comes built onto a specially made truck, and its ease of setup and reliability far outweigh the premium rental price.

topper: This is a **flag** placed by **grips** above and in front of a **movie light**, creating a big shadow on the wall, most often to hide a nasty **boom shadow**. If a light is spraying light beams all over the place, it might get a bottomer and a side-er, as well.

touch-up: Minute alterations in **star's** hair and makeup undertaken at the last minute to infuriate the already anxious **producer** and **DP**. Touch-ups are necessary after any break longer than a minute or two, in order to ensure **continuity** with previously filmed **shots**. It also gives the stars a chance to feel pampered.

track: (1) Shiny metal miniature railroad track on which the **dolly** travels during movie photography, assembled and leveled by the **grips**.

(2) During a **shot,** moving the camera dolly, left, right, in, out, it doesn't matter—it's all referred to as tracking. Moving cameras add a dynamic presence to films; for example, have a look at Stanley Kubrick's masterpiece *The Shining*. The **Steadicam** tracking through the haunted house pulls the audience into the story by putting them (visually) behind the wheel of the child's tricycle. On the **set,** good tracking shots require a bit of planning and rehearsal. See also **crane** and **remote head**.

trailer: (1) Every movie filming on **location** will have two to five Winnebago RV trailers for use by the **stars** and the **director**. The stars use them to hide from an adoring public, and while waiting for the

DP to finish the lighting. The director uses them to hide from the **producer,** who is wondering, "Why the hell aren't we shooting!?"

(2) **Previews** of coming attractions are called trailers, because in the old days they came after the **feature** presentation. Cartoons and short films came before the main attraction, in the spot now occupied by Mountain Dew commercials and lame slide shows advertising local businesses.

translight: This is a really, really big transparency (slide photograph) hung behind a **set** to serve as a **background**. Most often this is a cityscape seen through a window. Just don't walk in front of the translight while the camera is filming—you'll look like King Kong.

transportation captain: King of the **teamsters,** responsible for the safe transportation of the equipment and people during **production**. Tells the trucks when to move out, kinda like John Wayne in that movie: "Take 'em to Missouri! Yehaa!"

treatment: A one-page synopsis of a **script** sent to **producers** and **directors** who can't be bothered to read the full hundred pages.

tripod: Large adjustable three-legged stationary **camera** support, really just a heavy-duty version of the one you may have at home, except the movie version has sharp spikes on the bottom of the feet. They come in regular and baby sizes, and are very versatile. Once I saw a **director** use one to skewer an unsuspecting rattlesnake while on **location** in Wyoming for *Wild Horses,* starring Kenny Rogers.

trombone: (1) A twisted bit of pipe used by the **best boy** to hang a light on the edge of a **set**. "Hand me a **blonde** on a trombone!"

(2) *Trombone* as a derogatory term can refer to a tendency to overuse the **zoom** lens by **hack** directors. Smart-ass **crew** people will secretly make the sliding trombone motion.

t-stop: Movie **lenses** are marked in these cryptic transmission-stop numbers instead of the Nikon camera's more common **f-stops,**

which determine how much light will be reaching the film during **exposure**. Changing the t-stop can have a big effect on the way the film ultimately looks, and is left up to the **DP**.

tungsten: Movie lighting gear is neatly divided into two groups. Daylight (blue) and tungsten (orange), named for the chemical makeup of the filament and bulb of the lamp. Daylight instruments are used as **fill lights** when filming in sunlight outdoors, and indeed anytime you need large, powerful **HMI** lighting. When shooting **interiors** or night **exteriors**, tungsten lighting instruments are often used, as there is a wide assortment of these traditional movie lamps available, they're cheap, and the light they produce (slightly orange) balances well with motion picture film.

turkey: Unprofitable film. Flop. Bomb. See any recent film starring Ben Affleck.

turn around, turnaround: (1) In L.A., this phrase describes a **scriptwriter's** purgatory, wherein a change in **studio** heads results in the suspension of all the former boss's pet projects in development but not yet filming, including your project. "My film is in turnaround!"

(2) On working movie **sets**, turning around means the next planned **shot** will look in the opposite direction. All the support equipment—**props**, lights, **flags**, **camera** gear—will need to be moved to a new **staging area** behind the new camera position to stay out of the new shot. See **taco cart**.

(3) Yet a third meaning for *turnaround* is the time between when work finishes (**wrap**) and **call time** the next day, ten hours being the usual minimum turnaround, though sometimes this shrinks to eight hours in a pinch. "You can sleep when you're dead!"

turn over: *Turn over* means "turn on the bloody camera" to a British film **crew.**

twelve-step: Not a self-help program at all, but rather a ladder with twelve rungs, each spaced one foot apart. Lots of ladders are carried by the **grips,** and they're cleverly identified by the number of steps (four-step, ten-step, and so on).

twenty-by: Twenty-foot-square aluminum pipe **frames** are erected by the **grips** to hold **silks** and are used to soften direct overhead sunlight. Twenty-by black fabric can be used to create giant shadow areas. When a big gust of wind slides across the **set,** the **grips** hold down the twenty-bys, and the rest of the **cast** and **crew** duck or scatter.

two shot: Simple. A two-shot is a picture featuring two **actors,** as opposed to a **single.**

two-tees: This is the commonly used (and politically incorrect) description of a **close-up** showing an **actress** that features her—well, her cleavage, her two-tees. Hey, I didn't coin these terms; I'm just passing 'em along.

Tyler mount: Hollywood engineering wizard Nelson Tyler invented a **camera** mount for helicopters that bears his name. (He also reportedly invented rocket-powered flying backpacks that actually work great . . . at least on the way up! A controlled landing proved to be a slight problem, as did scorched blue jeans.)

ubangi: A long "lip" attached to the **dolly** in order to extend the reach of the **boom**. Named for the African tribe who are famous for extending their lips with huge colorful wooden plates. This might be the next way for American teens to torture their parents, after tattoos and multiple piercing become mundane.

undercrank: If one were to adjust the movie **camera's** filming speed from the standard twenty-four frames per second (fps), downward to 18 or 12 fps, it is termed *undercranking*. The resulting images speed by in fast motion when projected, just like early Keystone Kops comedies, which were indeed originally filmed at 18 fps. These days, one might use a little judicious undercranking to help a **stunt** in need of a dynamic boost.

underwater housing: An underwater housing is a metal or plastic watertight box, into which the movie or video camera is placed. This facilitates filming on a **wet set**, or even well below the surface. Underwater shooting is much more time consuming and generally less convenient than conventional filming. Communication with **directors** and **actors** is hard enough on dry land. Don't forget, *Jaws* went way over budget.

union: For **Hollywood** movies, the **IA** is the union covering all the **grip, electric, camera, sound,** and **prop** crews. Anyone working thirty days on a film has the right to join the union (and gain access to more work), but you need to be *in* the crafts union to get onto the **set** in the first place. **Directors** have the **DGA**, and **screenwriters** have the WGA, but these are guilds, a fancier name for unions.

UPM: Unit Production Manager. Forget about all the **executive producers, producers, associate producers**—the UPM is the person making sure the movie work gets done. Scheduling, hiring and firing people, renting truckloads of gear, arranging a catered lunch for 125 hungry **crew**—someone does all this work, and that someone is the UPM.

up front: The opposite of **back end**. Most **star actors** receive all their salary in an up-front deal, before filming starts.

upstage: A stage direction given by the **director** to an **actor** meaning "walk farther away from the camera." In the dark days before movies, there was live theater, and the stages sloped down toward the front. To upstage another actor, all you had to do was take a step backwards, and you would appear taller and more commanding.

vanity production: Producers and **directors** make the movies, but when **stars** reach a certain prominence, the balance of power shifts. **Studios** want to keep big stars happy, so they set them up in bungalow offices peopled with **readers, screenwriters,** and **associate producer** types. Meetings are held, **scripts** are written and rewritten, costs are deducted, everyone is happy. Occasionally, a pretty good movie will be the result, such as *Dances with Wolves* for Kevin Costner's TiG Productions, or *Charlie's Angels* for Drew Barrymore's Flower Films.

vanities: Term occasionally used by the technical **crew (grips, electrics, camera department)** to describe the folks in charge of **hair and makeup.**

VFX: Visual effects. Pictures of spaceships, aliens, dinosaurs, for instance. A specialized **crew** creates these images after **principal photography** has long since been **in the can.**

video assist: Some of the light coming through the **lens** in a movie film **camera** is redirected via mirrors to the **camera operator's** eyepiece, and some goes to the video assist. A miniature video camera is affixed alongside the camera eyepiece, and a monitor is placed in **video village** that enables the **director** to see the **shot,** the

script supervisor to spot potential errors, and the **actors** to gaze at themselves.

video playback: Beloved by **actors** and **directors**, hated by **UPMs** on a tight budget, video playback enables the repeated viewing of previously filmed **takes**. If there is any sort of problem, the irony is that it is quicker to shoot an additional take right away than to continually consult the videotape. Fans of the NFL, with its referee video review, know what I'm talking about.

video transfer: See **film-to-tape**. This is the process that converts the original film in the movie **camera** to digital videotape.

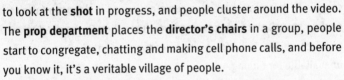

video village: Having a video monitor on a film **set** is like a magnet, second only to the **craft service** table. Everyone wants to look at the **shot** in progress, and people cluster around the video. The **prop department** places the **director's chairs** in a group, people start to congregate, chatting and making cell phone calls, and before you know it, it's a veritable village of people.

VistaVision: This was one of many attempts in the 1950s to improve the quality of **wide-screen** film presentation. (See **Cinerama**.) In VistaVision, the film winds through the camera sideways, yielding a 100 percent increase in imaging area. If you ever have the opportunity to view an original VistaVision **print** in a real theater, RUN, do not walk, to the ticket booth. Many of the later films of the great Alfred Hitchcock were filmed in VistaVision. These films have a clarity and sharpness that make the new *Spider-Man* look like a cheesy video game.

visual effects: These are distinct from **practical effects,** which are created live on **set**. Visual effects are added after the fact by  computer whizzes from companies like Digital Domain or **ILM** months after **principal photography** is finished.

visual effects supervisor: As movies have become more effects-laden, the job of the FX supervisor has assumed greater importance. Most of the work centers around **models** and computers operating in darkened rooms during **postproduction.** During **principal photography,** he or she occasionally makes an appearance on **set** to "supervise."

voice-over: A VO is an **actor** or narrator speaking from **offscreen**. One example of this is a VO of a private detective in a typical **film noir**. ("I knew she would stop at nothing to get the Maltese Falcon. . . .") Voice-overs are also commonly used in **documentaries** to explain **story points** not covered in pictures. Ken Burns used VO extensively in *The Civil War,* as many of the original participants were unavailable for filming.

waist shot: (As opposed to *waste shot,* which is the kind of photography that ends up on the **cutting-room floor**.) A waist shot is a **medium shot** including the **actor's** head, shoulders, and belly—the bottom **edge of frame** cuts him at the waist. Variations of this shot with more colorful names include the **two tees** and the **cowboy**.

walk and talk: A **shot** where two characters—that's right, you guessed it—walk and talk. That makes it sound easy, but it's not. Often there are a dozen **crew** people scurrying ahead, carrying **cables, mics,** and heavy **cameras**. The trick is for the **actors** to walk slow and talk fast.

walkaway: (1) This can refer to a one-hour meal break with no food provided by the **producer**. (Walk away, and find your own damn **lunch!**)

(2) *Walkaway* also refers to a **location** where you can simply leave the **cameras** and lights in place for the next day's work at **wrap**. This is much more efficient than packing and unpacking the equipment trucks each day during a **load-in**.

walkie: Handheld walkie-talkie radio transceivers are carried by many of the working **crew** to help coordinate all aspects of the film. **PAs** carry walkies to help them round up **extras**, keep **bogies** off the **set**, and direct people to **craft service**. **Grips** and **electrics** use them for interdepartmental communications. ("Bring me the freakin' **dolly**, *now!*") The **director** may be artistically in charge of the film, but the **AD** facilitates the work by addressing the crew on walkie channel number 1.

wallstretcher: Pipe or wooden board installed by the **riggers** in a **practical location** near the ceiling to support lights and other movie impedimenta. Sometimes a room heats up, and the gear can shift around a little. Make sure that wallstretcher stays up there! Better to ruin somebody's wallpaper than to drop one hundred pounds of hot lights on my head. (Hey, it's happened!)

watch your back: A movie **set** is a busy place, crowded with **grips**, camerapeople, **producers**, **actors**, drivers, chefs, masseuses, and the like. When you need to charge through the crowd with a large piece of moviemaking equipment, the proper warning is "Watch your back!" Other phrases with which one can clear a wide path include **"Hot points!" "Clear!"** and "Move—or bleed!"

we're in, or **we're back in:** This is an **AD** phrase you hear relayed over the **walkies** every day. It means roughly, "According to *my* watch, it's time to get to work! Move it!"

wedge: Sections of **dolly track** placed on uneven ground are leveled with temporary wooden wedges, or thin housing shingles (*shims* or *cribbing*) placed underneath. In Germany, **crews** sometimes resort to another readily available shim material: thin cardboard beer coasters. Hey, whatever works.

weekend: This relatively recent term is used by **producers** to describe a film's opening-weekend box office receipts, generally a good indicator of potential future profits, expressed in American dollars and the number of theaters showing the film. For example, *The Passion of the Christ II: The Resurrection* did $28 million, on 2,600 screens!

Western dolly: This is a primitive wheeled conveyance that supports the camera and rolls on large balloon pneumatic tires. They're hard to steer, but are great for rolling across the desert sand filming Lee Marvin, John Wayne, or Rin Tin Tin. A smaller version is the **doorway dolly**.

wet down: Sometimes a movie **company** contracts with a water truck to hose down the street just prior to filming. This is popular when shooting in urban areas at night, as the water on the ground reflects all the storefronts and streetlights. Check out any film by **director** Michael Mann, including the 1981 film *Thief,* starring James Caan. The whole film looks as though a torrential rainstorm has just ended.

wet set: It doesn't have to be James Cameron's *The Abyss,* but any **scene** in standing water is called a wet set. I've worked on several, and I can say the following without qualification: (1) Water is always colder than you anticipate. (Don't forget, it's a twelve-hour **workday**.) (2) The warming hot tub is only for the movie **stars**—now get back to work! (3) Really expensive dry suits are more comfortable than clammy, cold, cheapo wet suits. Before filming, ask the **producer** to buy one for you. (Hint: Use the word *safety.*)

whip pan: Sometimes called a *swish pan,* a whip pan is when the **camera operator** quickly re-aims the film camera between two separate subjects in a continuous **shot.** An overused technique on **music videos** as well as action films from the 1970s. See also **snap zoom.**

white balance: Movie lighting and **grip crews** spend a lot of time balancing the colors of all the lights on a film **set.** On a professional video **shoot,** all one has to do is briefly hold a white card in front of the **lens,** hit the button on the **camera** labeled WHITE BALANCE, and you're good to go. Your home digital and video camera generally white-balance automatically. If a film crew wants a sunset or a moonlight effect, it's time to get out the **filters.**

wide angle: A **lens** that sees more (a wider field of view) than the human eye. That's the standard definition, but in reality people's eyes scan around quite a bit, and the brain reassembles the many individual pictures into a coherent whole. You're doing it right now! The opposite of wide angle is **telephoto.**

wide screen: (1) Movies photographed for **theatrical release.** See **aspect ratio.**

(2) This is also the designation for movies on tape and DVD shown in the superior **letterbox** format; they've avoided the **pan-and-scan** process. The opposite of wide screen would be **full screen,** but you'll see the movie just as it was first shown in the theater if you opt for the wide-screen letterbox version instead.

window: The last shot on the day's **call sheet** is eagerly anticipated by **cast** and **crew,** and nicknames include *window, LFS,* and *martini*. The last shot is called the window because you can see through it, to **wrap**.

Winnie: Winnebago. See **trailer**.

wireless mic: Often in addition to using a **boom pole**, the sound **mixer** will resort to placing small wireless radio microphones under the **actor's** clothing. This can lead to some familiarity between the sound technician and the **thespian**, and presents difficulties when the **scene** calls for intimate apparel, such as a bikini. Where does one hide the **mic** and its power supply? I leave it to your imagination.

workday: Movies typically **shoot** for twelve to sixteen hours a day. No kidding. When the average corporate executive is heading home, the film **crew** is probably thinking about a half-hour **lunch** break. The economics are easy to understand. If J. Lo gets a half million per week, the **producer** will shoot around the clock and hire her for only eight weeks instead of ten. Congratulations, you've saved a million bucks! Additional salary and overtime for longer technician **workdays** are small in comparison. Movie crews work long hours, defer sleep until weekends, and depend on nearly toxic levels of caffeine to remain alert.

working title: Movies can sink or swim based on the title up on the theater marquee, and when inspiration takes a holiday, the **producer** temporarily slaps any old name on the **slate**. I've worked on several films with working titles different from the movie's ultimate name, *Big Daddy (Guy Gets Kid)*, *Return to Paradise (Force Majeure)*, and *Hitch (The Last First Kiss)*, to name three. I hear *Star Wars* was originally titled *Darth . . . and Friends!*, but that's just a rumor.

works: When planning a scene, after a brief **line-up**, the **AD** running the **set** will request that the **actors** head to "the works" while the lighting and **grip crew** prepare for the next **shot**. This is a lot like the Cowardly Lion visiting the groomers in the Emerald City in *The Wizard of Oz* (with a snip-snip here, and a snip-snip there!). The actors will visit in turn the costuming, hair, and makeup **departments**. They'll return to the set when the **DP** announces the lighting is finished and "We're ready for **first team!**"

wrangler: The person in charge of training, coaching, and chasing down the bears, dogs, cats, and other animals who perform in films. They may train the animals for months in advance. During filming, the wrangler will be hiding just out of **camera** range, hoping his highly trained pet gorilla hits the **mark** and refrains from ripping the co-star's arms off.

wrap: At the end of another magic **Hollywood** movie **workday**, the **AD** will call out, "It's a wrap, people! **Call time** is six a.m. for the **crew!**" **Wrapping** means "putting the gear away and heading home." Or better yet, get an assistant to put the equipment away, and sneak off ten minutes early. Just don't forget to grab a **call sheet**.

wrap gift: At the conclusion of **principal photography**, the **producer**, or sometimes the **star**, will give gifts to the **crew**, such as a duffle bag or a **crew jacket**. One quiet morning a few days before Christmas, I received a chocolate cake baked by a group of inner-city reformed gang members. It took several readings of the card, signed *Dusty*, to figure out that Dustin Hoffman (whom I've never met) must have gotten my name from a crew list on Costa-Gavras's film *Mad*

City and included me in the spirit of holiday giving. Nice. My friends are all impressed each and every time I remind them that Dustin Hoffman once sent me a cake for Christmas. Dusty, I call him.

writer: See also **screenwriter**. Why are so many names listed as "writer" in movie **credits**, you ask? **Producers** and **directors** like to rewrite **screenplays** right up to, and even during, shooting. If there's a problem, extra writers are quickly hired, sometimes to "fix" specific scenes. For example, on *What About Bob?* director Frank Oz received newly rewritten script pages via fax on the **set** each morning. Once a movie is finished and looks like a hit, you'll see everyone maneuvering around, trying to land a writing **credit**. On the other hand, if the film bombs, people may try to take their names off the project, which is termed an *orphan*. See **Alan Smithee**.

zoom: Every home video shooter knows how to hit the button to zoom in—that is, to bring the subject closer with the **lens**. As with any new toy or special effect, filmmakers initially tended to overdo it. Unnecessary zooms were everywhere in the movies from the late '60s to early '70s. These days, every movie has to include at least two slow-motion, Hong Kong–style flying kick-fight scenes. At least two.

zoom lens: A **lens** with variable **focal length**, first developed by **Hollywood** cameraman Joseph Walker. Essential for sports coverage and newsgathering, when the cameraperson wants to maintain some distance from the subject (such as burning buildings and crashing cars!). On movies, zoom lenses are typically used for convenience, in order to avoid the brief downtime associated with changing large fragile lenses with fixed **focal lengths**. See **prime lenses**.

—

That's a *wrap*. I'll see you on
the next big one!

DAVE KNOX COMPLETE FILMOGRAPHY

1984

Maria's Lovers—Steadicam Operator (Dir. Andrei Konchalovsky, starring Nastassja Kinski, John Savage)

Body Rock—Steadicam Operator (Dir. Marcelo Epstein, starring Lorenzo Lamas)

Threesome—B Camera and Steadicam (Dir. Lou Antonio, starring Dana Delany, Stephen Collins)

Falling in Love—Steadicam Operator (Dir. Ulu Grosbard, starring Robert De Niro, Meryl Streep)

1985

Wild Horses—B Camera and Steadicam (Dir. Dick Lowry, starring Kenny Rogers, Pam Dawber)

The Toxic Avenger—Additional Camera Operator (Dir. Lloyd Kaufman and Michael Herz, starring Mitch Cohen)

1986

Adam's Apple—Steadicam Operator (Dir. James Frawley)

Seize the Day—Steadicam Operator (Dir. Fielder Cook, starring Robin Williams)

Off Beat—Steadicam Operator (Dir. Michael Dinner, starring Judge Reinhold, Meg Tilly)

Jumpin' Jack Flash—Steadicam Operator (Dir. Penny Marshall, starring Whoopi Goldberg, Annie Potts)

Quiet Cool—B Camera and Steadicam Operator (Dir. Clay Borris, starring James Remar)

1987

Dirty Dancing—Steadicam Operator (Dir. Emile Ardolino, starring Patrick Swayze, Jennifer Grey)

Square Dance—Steadicam Operator (Dir. Daniel Petrie, starring Winona Ryder, Jason Robards)

Highlander—Steadicam Operator (Dir. Russell Mulcahy, starring Christopher Lambert, Sean Connery)

Hiding Out—Steadicam Operator (Dir. Bob Giraldi, starring Jon Cryer, Annabeth Gish)

1988

Tougher Than Leather—Director of Photography, reshoots (Dir. Rick Rubin, starring Run-DMC)

Spenser: For Hire—B Camera and Steadicam Operator (Various Directors, starring Robert Urich)

Short Circuit 2—B Camera and Steadicam Operator (Dir. Kenneth Johnson, starring Michael McKean)

Superboy—Steadicam Operator (Dir. Kenneth Bowser, starring John Haymes Newton, Stacy Haiduk)

1989

Sea of Love—B Camera and Steadicam (Dir. Harold Becker, starring Al Pacino, Ellen Barkin)

Black Rain—Additional Steadicam (Dir. Ridley Scott, starring Michael Douglas, Andy Garcia)

The Dream Team—B Camera and Steadicam Operator (Dir. Howard Zieff, starring Michael Keaton)

Last Exit to Brooklyn—Steadicam (Dir. Uli Edel, starring Jennifer Jason Leigh, Burt Young)

1990

Exorcist III—Steadicam Operator (Dir. William Peter Blatty, starring George C. Scott)

State of Grace—Steadicam Operator (Dir. Phil Joanou, starring Sean Penn, Robin Wright Penn)

Rocky V—Additional Camera Operator (Dir. John G. Avildsen, starring Sylvester Stallone, Talia Shire)

Luther the Geek—Director of Photography (Dir. Carlton J. Albright, starring Joan Roth, Edward Terry)

1991

The Silence of the Lambs—Steadicam Operator, uncredited (Dir. Jonathan Demme, starring Jodie Foster)

The Hard Way—B Camera and Steadicam operator (Dir. John Badham, starring Michael J. Fox, James Woods)

What about Bob?—Steadicam Operator (Dir. Frank Oz, starring Bill Murray, Richard Dreyfuss)

True Identity—B Camera and Steadicam Operator (Dir. Charles Lane, starring Lenny Henry, Frank Langella)

Dead and Alive: The Race for Gus Farace—Steadicam Operator (Dir. Peter Markle, starring Tony Danza, Dan Lauria)

One Good Cop—Steadicam Operator (Dir. Heywood Gould, starring Michael Keaton, Rene Russo)

Soapdish—Steadicam Operator (Dir. Michael Hoffman, starring Sally Field, Kevin Kline)

Necessary Roughness—B Camera and Steadicam (Dir. Stan Dragoti, starring Scott Bakula, Hector Elizondo)

Billy Bathgate—Steadicam Operator (Dir. Robert Benton, starring Dustin Hoffman, Nicole Kidman)

1992

Quiet Killer—Additional Director of Photography (Dir. Sheldon Larry, starring Kate Jackson)

Glengarry Glen Ross—Steadicam Operator (Dir. James Foley, starring Jack Lemmon, Al Pacino, Alan Arkin)

The Last of the Mohicans—Steadicam Operator, uncredited (Dir. Michael Mann, starring Daniel Day-Lewis)

Scent of a Woman—B Camera and Steadicam Operator (Dir. Martin Brest, starring Al Pacino, Chris O'Donnell)

Light Sleeper—Steadicam Operator (Dir. Paul Shrader, starring Willem Dafoe, Susan Sarandon)

That Night—B Camera and Steadicam (Dir. Craig Bolotin, starring Juliette Lewis, C. Thomas Howell)

Night and the City—Steadicam Operator (Dir. Irwin Winkler, starring Robert De Niro, Jessica Lange)

1993

Family Pictures—Camera Operator (Dir. Philip Saville, starring Anjelica Huston, Sam Neill, Kyra Sedgwick)

Weekend at Bernies II—Steadicam Operator (Dir. Robert Klane, starring Andrew McCarthy)

The Age of Innocence—Steadicam Operator, uncredited (Dir. Martin Scorsese, starring Winona Ryder, Daniel Day-Lewis)

Six Degrees of Separation—Steadicam Operator (Dir. Fred Schepisi, starring Stockard Channing, Will Smith)

1994

Water Ride—Director of Photography (Dir. Lane Smith, starring Bill Irwin)

Fresh—Camera Operator (Dir. Boaz Yakin, starring Samuel Jackson, Giancarlo Esposito)

Car 54, Where Are You?—2nd Unit Camera Operator (Dir. Bill Fishman, starring David Johansen)

Above the Rim—B Camera Operator (Dir. Jeff Pollack, starring Tupac Shakur, Leon)

With Honors—Steadicam Operator (Dir. Alek Keshishian, starring Brendan Fraser, Joe Pesci)

1995

Smoke—Camera Operator (Dir. Wayne Wang, starring Harvey Keitel, William Hurt)

Blue in the Face—Camera Operator (Dir. Wayne Wang and Paul Auster, starring Harvey Keitel, Lou Reed, Roseanne)

Jumanji—Camera Operator (Dir. Joe Johnston, starring Robin Williams, Bonnie Hunt)

1996

City Hall—B Camera Operator (Dir. Harold Becker, starring Al Pacino, John Cusack)

Before and After—Steadicam Operator (Dir. Barbet Schroeder, starring Meryl Streep, Liam Neeson)

Grace of My Heart—2nd Unit Camera (Dir. Allison Anders, starring Illeana Douglas, Patsy Kensit)

Daylight—Camera Operator (Dir. Rob Cohen, starring Sylvester Stallone)

Luxor—Additional Director of Photography (Dir. Douglas Trumbull)

The Associate—Steadicam Operator (Dir. Don Petrie, starring Whoopi Goldberg)

Marvin's Room—Camera Operator, reshoots (Dir. Jerry Zaks, starring Meryl Streep, Diane Keaton)

One Fine Day—Steadicam Operator (Dir. Michael Hoffman, starring George Clooney, Michelle Pfeiffer)

I'm Not Rappaport—Camera Operator (Dir. Herb Gardner, starring Walter Matthau, Ossie Davis)

Ransom—2nd Unit Operator (Dir. Ron Howard, starring Mel Gibson, Rene Russo)

The Ring—Steadicam Operator (Dir. Armand Mastroianni, starring Michael York, Nastassja Kinski)

1997

The Devil's Own—B Camera Operator (Dir. Alan J. Pakula, starring Harrison Ford, Brad Pitt)

8 Heads in a Duffle Bag—2nd Unit Director of Photography (Dir. Tom Schulman, starring Joe Pesci)

Julian Po—Steadicam Operator (Dir. Alan Wade, starring Christian Slater)

Mad City—Camera Operator (Dir. Costa-Gavras, starring John Travolta, Dustin Hoffman)

Feds—2nd Unit Director of Photography (Dir. John David Coles, starring Blair Brown)

In & Out—Additional Camera Operator (Dir. Frank Oz, starring Kevin Kline, Matt Dillon)

Brooklyn South—2nd Unit Director of Photography (Dir. Paris Barclay, starring James Sikking, Yancy Butler)

Jungle 2 Jungle—Steadicam Operator (Dir. John Pasquin, starring Tim Allen, Martin Short)

Night Falls on Manhattan—B Camera Operator (Dir. Sidney Lumet, starring Andy Garcia, Lena Olin)

1998

When It's Over—Director of Photography (Dir. Richard Mancuso, starring Troy Ruptash, Vincent Caruso)

Wide Awake—Camera Operator (Dir. M. Night Shyamalan, starring Dana Delany, Dennis Leary)

Return to Paradise—Camera Operator (Dir. Joseph Ruben, starring Vince Vaughan, Joaquin Phoenix)

Storefront Hitchcock—B Camera Operator (Dir. Jonathan Demme, starring Robyn Hitchcock)

54—Camera Operator, reshoots (Dir. Mark Christopher, starring Neve Campbell, Salma Hayek)

1999

Virus—Camera Operator (Dir. John Bruno, starring Jamie Lee Curtis, Donald Sutherland)

In Dreams—Steadicam Operator (Dir. Neil Jordan, starring Annette Benning, Aidan Quinn)

Big Daddy—Camera Operator (Dir. Dennis Dugan, starring Adam Sandler, Joey Lauren Adams)

Mad About You—Camera Operator (Dir. Michael Lembeck, starring Paul Reiser, Helen Hunt)

King of Queens—Camera Operator (Dir. Rob Schiller, starring Kevin James, Leah Remini)

2000

Overnight Sensation—Director of Photography (Dir. Glen Trotiner, starring Maxwell Caulfield)

Beautiful Joe—2nd Unit Director of Photography (Dir. Stephen Metcalfe, starring Sharon Stone)

The Adventures of Rocky and Bullwinkle—2nd Unit Camera Operator (Dir. Des McAnuff, starring Jason Alexander, Rene Russo)

Isn't She Great—B Camera Operator (Dir. Andrew Bergman, starring Nathan Lane, Bette Midler)

Mary and Rhoda—Camera Operator (Dir. Barnet Kellman, starring Mary Tyler Moore, Valerie Harper)

Cruel Intentions 2—Camera Operator 2nd Unit (Dir. Roger Kumble, starring Mimi Rogers, Robin Dunne)

Bull—Camera Operator (Dir. Allan Arkush, starring Malik Yoba, Stanley Tucci)

The $treet—B Camera Operator (Dir. Michael Dinner, starring Bridgette Wilson, Jennifer Connelly)

2001

3 A.M.—Camera Operator (Dir. Lee Davis, starring Danny Glover, Pam Grier)

The Devil and Daniel Webster—Camera Operator (Dir. Alec Baldwin, starring Anthony Hopkins, Jennifer Love Hewitt)

Down—Camera Operator (Dir. Dick Maas, starring Naomi Watts, James Marshall)

Double Whammy—Credit Sequence Director of Photography (Dir. Tom DiCillo, starring Elizabeth Hurley)

Swimfan—Additional Camera Operator (Dir. John Polson, starring Erika Christensen, Jesse Bradford)

2002

New Americans—Director of Photography (Dir. Allen Blumberg, starring Omar Metwally, Justin Reinsilber)

Paid in Full—Camera Operator (Dir. Charles Stone III, starring Mekhi Phifer, Wood Harris)

Empire—Additional Camera Operator (Dir. Franc. Reyes, starring Fat Joe, John Leguizamo)

Will & Grace—Camera Operator (Dir. James Burrows, starring Eric McCormack, Debra Messing)

Bad Company—Additional Camera Operator (Dir. Joel Schumacher, starring Chris Rock)

Rollerball—Additional Camera Operator (Dir. John McTiernan, starring LL Cool J, Rebecca Romjin-Stamos)

City by the Sea—B Camera Operator (Dir. Michael Caton-Jones, starring Robert De Niro)

2003

Cold Case—Camera Operator (Dir. James Witmore Jr., starring Kathryn Morris, John Finn)

NYPD Blue—Camera Operator (Dir. Mark Tinker, starring Dennis Franz, Gordon Clapp)

It Runs in the Family—Additional Camera Operator (Dir. Fred Schepisi, starring Kirk and Michael Douglas)

Frozen Impact—Camera Operator (Dir. Neil Kinsella, starring Linda Purl, Ted McGinley)

Rudy: The Rudy Giuliani Story—Camera Operator (Dir. Robert Dornhelm, starring James Woods)

Killer Flood: The Day the Dam Broke—Camera Operator (Dir. Doug Campbell, starring Bruce Boxleitner, Michele Green)

2004

House of D—Camera Operator (Dir. David Duchovny, starring Robin Williams, Téa Leoni, David Duchovny)

The Manchurian Candidate—Additional Camera Operator (Dir. Jonathan Demme, starring Denzel Washington)

In Good Company—2nd Unit Director of Photography (Dir. Paul Weitz, starring Dennis Quaid)

Hack—2nd Unit Director of Photography (Creator David Koepp, starring David Morse)

2005

Hitch—Camera Operator (Dir. Andy Tennant, starring Will Smith, Eva Mendes, Kevin James)

Blind Justice—A Camera Operator (Dir. Gary Fleder, John Badham, starring Ron Eldard)

The Honeymooners—Additional Operator (Dir. John Schultz, starring Cedric the Entertainer)

Carlito's Way: The Beginning—B Camera Operator (Dir. Michael Bregman, starring Sean "P. Diddy" Combs)